Audio Book Release Announcement:
"Liao-Fan's Four Lessons"

The book "Liao-Fan's Four Lessons" was written in 1603 by Yuan Huang Hun Kun to teach his son the proper way to conduct one's life. Master Yin-Kuang, the now deceased Thirteenth Patriarch of the Pure Land School, had distributed, along with his missionaries, over a million copies of this book and he had never ceased encouraging people to study, practice and give lectures on this book, Our teacher Master Chin-Kung has also advised us to promote this book widely so that everyone will firmly understand the cause and effect of our actions. It is only by distancing ourselves form cruelty and cultivating kindness we can resolve and eliminate the disasters that our world is facing.

Acting on his advice, over the past three years, our Society has made audio book versions of this wonderful book in Mandarin, Taiwanese, Hakka, and Cantoncse. A children's edition is also available, Recently we asked The Amitabha Buddhist Society of Malaysia to produce an English edition of this audio book. Since its release, it has been accepted as having attained an international standard that will appeal to English speaking countries and to those who are learning English.

For overseas Chinese who are unfamiliar with the

Chinese culture, this English audio book is an easy introduction to the Chinese culture, We hope that the wide distribution of "Liao-Fan's Four Lessons" will help to spread the message of Buddha's Dharrna to every corner of the world, like bamboo shoots sprouting from the earth after rain. Everyone will become kindhearted, say kind things, do kind deeds and become a good person. In short, when "the heart is pure the nation will become pure; when the heart is peaceful the world will become peaceful."

It is our sincere hope that your Society willl join us in achieving this noble goal. You can help by reproducing this audio book and distributing copies all over the world. The message contained in this audio book will help to reduce the disasters facing our world, if not eradicating them from our world completely.

Together, we can promote and spread this noble cause!

 Wishing you peace and tranquillity.

Note: Please us the C.D. version as master copy when you reproduce this audio book, This will avoid sound quality deterioration during the recording process.

Liao-Fan's Work Team

Preface

The book of Liao Fan's Four Lessons is not only widely read among the learned families of China and treasured by them as a family heirloom, it has also borne long and profound influence on Japan's political and economic administrations.

The famous Japanese Han scholar, Yasuoko Masahiro is an ardent promoter of this book. He has suggested that the Emperor of Japan and every Japanese Prime Minister to treat this book as a national treasure and that they should memorize the lessons, read them diligently and understand the lessons given in the book thoroughly. Anyone who wishes to govern should study the book carefully.

Yasuoko Masahiro praised this book as "a magnificent knowledge that can move one's life". This book has influenced the youths of Meiji era greatly, has left its mark in China since four hundred years ago and has deeply impressed upon the Japanese society since one hundred years ago. Liao Fan's Four Lessons is a good book worthy of repeated studies by youths as well as anyone who strives to do better on their lives.

Liao Fan's Four Lessons is divided into four chapters. If one takes 20 minutes each day to read one chapter, this book can be finished in four days. If one reads this book continuously for one year, he will be able to understand deeply the meanings within. This book also comes with explanatory footnotes and contemporary Chinese literary translation for easy reading.

袁了凡居士年譜　　了凡四訓研究學會編輯小組

1535 明世宗		1	袁了凡先生，名黃，字坤儀；江南吳江人。
嘉靖14年乙未			
1549~1550	乙酉	15	童年喪父。學醫。遇孔公。禮郁海谷先生為師。
	庚戌	16	縣考十四名……
1567 明穆宗			
隆慶元年 丁卯		33	殷秋溟宗師，申文准貢。入燕都（北京）。
1569			
	己巳	35	遊南雍。訪雲谷禪師。……改號了凡。
1570	庚午	36	禮部考科舉，算該第三，忽考第一。
			秋闈（八月）中式。
1571	辛未	37	丁敬宇賓，極其謙虛。……果中式。
			了凡先生進京會試，未中。
1577 明神宗			
萬曆五年 丁丑		43	與馮開之同處，其虛己斂容……會試第一（狀元）。
			了凡先生進京會試，未中。
1579	己卯	45	三十五，直歲發願至四十五歲，歷十餘年，
			三千善事才完成。……明年，竟東塔禪堂迴向。
1580	庚辰	46	庚辰南還。……起求子願，亦許行三千善事。
1581	辛巳	47	生男天啟，字匯，後亦成進士，終高要（廣東省）知縣。
1583	癸未	49	八月，三千之數已滿，……迴向。
			九月十三日，復起求進士願，許行善事一萬條。
1586	丙戌	52	登弟（成進士），授寶坻知縣（在河北省境內）。
			（按：孔先生算於寶坻某年，當選四川某縣知縣，
			未明登弟。五十三歲有厄，……是歲竟無恙。）
1586~1592			任職寶坻縣長。……只減糧一節，萬行俱完矣。
			（按：在寶坻縣當縣長者，非常注重人民的福利，
			興辦水利，開墾耕種，省諸雜役以便民。）
			五十八歲，了凡先生入京觀見神宗皇帝。
1593	癸巳	59	升拔為兵部職方司的主管。當時日寇侵犯朝鮮…
			（按：當時的經略（駐朝軍事長官）宋應昌聘了凡
			為軍諮書畫（並兼支援朝鮮的軍隊。後
			了凡被彈劾，在抬進（讒官）任內，引疾返鄉。
1603	癸卯	69	今六十九矣。（由此推知，了凡四訓，寫於此年。）
			（返鄉後，非常懇切、諄諄地行善。享年七十四歲。）
1608	戌申	74	先生非常喜歡研究學問，書不論古今，事不

2

分輕重，舉凡星象、法律、水利、理數、兵
備、政治。都非常通達。著有兩行齋集、曆
法新書、皇都水利、評注八代文宗、群書備
考、手批綱鑑等書。

1621～1627　　明嘉宗天啟年間，了凡的冤案終於真相大白，朝廷追敍
了凡征討日寇的功績，贈封他為尚寶司少卿。

參考資料：《了凡四訓》明‧袁了凡。《袁了凡居士傳白話》清‧彭紹升。《了凡四
訓今譯》民國‧陳慧劍校註。《大辭典‧中國歷史紀年》三民書局編。《靈芝律師年
譜》民國‧弘一律師撰。　1995年2月 顧生極樂僧　釋心雍 於埔里

ABOUT THIS EDITION

The English version tape-recorded books titles "Liao Fan's Four Lessons" are brought forth primarily to benefit the migrant Chinese who had settled down overseas and their younger generation who had slow and by inevitably becoming less and less familiar with the Chinese Culture; to introduce to them the Chinese Culture in a systemic manner,
simultaneously to propagate the right Dharma / Teachings of Buddha in the centres all over the world. With these readily packed tape-recorded materials and reference readings which come in handy, we trust and believe the Dharma / Teachings of Buddha would definitely bloom and blossom like the young bamboo shoots sprouting cheerfully out of the ground immediately upon the spring showers; and shall spread to each and every corner, each and every ethnic group around the world, bringing forth freedom to humanity and allaying unnecessary fear among people.

Last but not less, these shall provide as guiding principles to enable man to live their lives better, to handle matters better and ultimately to become better people; also to promote "A pure heart leads to p pure land, a peaceful mind leads to a peaceful world." As the basis and foundation of practicing and learning the Dharma / Teachings of Buddha to the fullest.

Liao-Fan's Four Lessons
Audio Book

Original Work by Mr. Liao-Fan Yuan of the Ming Dynasty
Interpreted by Mr. Zhi-Hai Huang
Re-edited by Liao-Fan's Work Team
Sponsored and recorded by The Foundation of Liao-Fan's Four Lessons

<u>Liao-Fan's Four Lessons</u> was originally written in the Ming Dynasty of China by Mr. Liao-Fan Yuan. The book was intended to teach his son, Tien-Chi Yuan, how to recognize the true face of destiny, how to tell good from evil, and the method for correcting one's faults and practicing kind deeds. It also provided living proof of the rewards and outcomes of people who practiced kind deeds and cultivated virtue and humility. Relating from his own experience at changing destiny, Mr. Yuan himself was a living embodiment of his teachings. After hearing this wonderful book, one may feel more open and confident towards life, and at the same time, courageously compelled to follow the example of Liao-Fan in changing one's original destiny. Liao-Fan's Four Lessons is truly a rare book which is not only

1

precious to an individual's spiritual needs, but is also capable of transforming unhealthy attitudes in today's society.

While listening through the lessons, one may wonder why the Chinese placed so much emphasis on examinations. In the olden days of Chinese civilization, studying was held in highest regard whilst all other occupations were considered low-class. The Chinese government selected its officials through a system of meritocracy; many levels of imperial examinations were given to all who wished to take them. It was very difficult to pass these tests, and one had to be very learned and talented in writing essays. Those who did pass had the chance to advance to high government positions and live a life of wealth and prominence. People who couldn't pass the examinations were not recognized, no matter how smart or able they were otherwise. That was the reason why many youths of that time turned to studying for the exams in hopes for a prosperous future.

Since the original work of Liao-Fan was written in classical Chinese, it tended to be poetic and terse, making the book hard to read and understand for modern-day people. In early 1900, Mr. Zhi-Hai Huang added a detailed commentary to the book using modern Chinese. This edition of Liao-Fan's Four Lessons became very popular and benefited many people of his time. However, as time went on, even Mr. Huang's edition became too tedious for today's readers, so the influence of this beneficial book was greatly reduced. In view of this sad situation, The Foundation of Liao-Fan's Four Lessons is devoted to the reorganization, editing, and reprinting of the book, allowing better access and understanding to these wonderful teachings. Today, with the sponsorship of kind people, this edition of The Brief Explanation of Liao-Fan's Four Lessons has been produced into Liao-Fan's Four Lessons Audio Book. After listening through it, we hope that everyone will learn the spirit of Liao-Fan in changing one's destiny and create a brighter future for oneself, the society, the nation, and all people of the world.

📖 The First Lesson: Learning To Create Destiny

(Narrator): *"Creating Destiny " is about forming one's fate rather than be bound by it. The Lesson of Learning to Create Destiny herein discusses the principle behind fate and the knowledge necessary to change it. By relating his own experience and trials at changing destiny, Mr. Liao-Fan Yuan taught his son, Tien-Chi not to be bound by fate, but rather to put forth his best effort in practicing kindness and cutting off evil. One should not reject doing a kind act simply because it seems to be a minute goodness, or commit an evil deed simply because it appears to be a small evil. If one practices in a proper manner, it is assured that one's destiny can be changed. It is often said, "Refraining from all evil and practicing all forms of kindness brings about the dispersion of disasters and the coming of fortune ". This is the principle behind creating one's destiny.*

(Liao-Fan): My father passed away when I was young, and mother persuaded me to learn medicine instead of becoming a scholar. Mother said to me:

(Mother): Learning medicine will be a good

4

way to support yourself and also to help others. Besides, having a skill on hand, you will never have to worry about making a living, and you can even become famous through your medical skills. This has always been an ambition your father had for you.

[Liao-Fan]: One day, at the Compassionate Cloud Temple, I met an elderly but distinguished looking man who had a long beard and had such a look of a sage that I immediately paid my respects to him. The old man told me:

[Old Man]: You are destined to become a government official. You can attain the rank of Erudite First Level Scholar next year, why aren't you studying for the exam?

[Liao-Fan]: So I told him of my mother's instructions to give up scholarly study for learning medicine. Then I asked for his name, birthplace, and residence. He replied:

[Old Man]: My last name is Kong. I came from <u>Yunnan</u> Province. I have inherited the knowledge of Mr. Shao, who developed the

5

art of prediction very well. By calculations, I'm supposed to pass it on to you.

[Liao-Fan]: Therefore, I led Mr. Kong to my home and told my mother about him. Mother told me to treat him well and said:

[Mother]: Since Mr. Kong is so good at predicting the future, he must also know our past. Let's ask him and test his authenticity.

[Liao-Fan]: As a result, I found Mr. Kong's calculations to be very accurate, even in very small cases. After hearing his words of advice, I once again thought about studying. I then consulted with my cousin Shen-chen. He recommended thus:

[Cousin]: "My friend, Mr. Hal-gu Yu is teaching at the home of Yo-fu Sheng. It would be very convenient for me to take you there for boarding and studying.

[Liao-Fan]: This was how I became Mr. Yu's student. Once again Mr. Kong made a prediction for me. He said:

[Mr. Kong]: As a student, you will place fourteenth in the county examination, seventy-first at the regional exam, and ninth at the provincial examination.

[Liao-Fan]: The following year, at the three places of examination, I placed exactly as he had predicted. Then Mr. Kong calculated the predictions for my entire life. He said:

[Mr. Kong]: You will pass such and such a test in such and such a year, you will become a civil servant in such a year, and in such a year you will get a promotion. Finally, you will be appointed as a magistrate in Szechuan Province. After holding that office for three and a half years, you will resign and return home. At the age of fifty-three, you will die around one o'clock in the morning on August 14th. It's a pity that you will not have a son.

[Liao-Fan]: I recorded and remembered all that he said. From then on, the outcome of every examination I took turned out exactly as Mr. Kong predicted. Mr. Kong also predicted that I would be promoted only after receiving a salary in the weight of ninety-one dans and five dous of rice. However, I had received only seventy-one dans of rice when the senior educational official Mr. Tu recommended me for a promotion. I secretly began to doubt Mr. Kong's predictions.

(Liao-Fan): Nevertheless, the prediction turned out to be correct after all, because the recommendation was turned down by Mr. Tu's superior, Mr. Yang. It was not until several years later when Mr. Chiu-min Ying saw my old exam papers and exclaimed:

(Mr. Ying): These five essays are as well written as reports to the Emperor! How can we bury the talents of such a great scholar?

(Liao-Fan): Mr. Ying wanted the magistrate to issue an official order for me to become a candidate for 'Imperial student' under his authority. After undergoing this eventful promotion, my calculations showed that I had received exactly ninety-one dans and five dous of rice. From then on, whether it was promotion, rank, or wealth, I deeply believed that all came in due time.

[Narrator]: Even the length of one's life is predestined.

[Liao-Fan]: I began to view everything in a more detached manner and ceased to seek gain and profit.

[Liao-Fan]: After being selected as an imperial student, I was to attend the university at Beijing. During my year-long stay at the capital, my interest in meditation grew and I often sat silently without giving rise to a single thought. I lost interest in books and did not study at all. Before I was to enter the national university at Nanking, I paid a visit to the enlightened Zen master Yun Gu at Chi-shia Mountain. We sat face to face in the Zen Hall for three days and nights without ever failing asleep. Master Yun Gu questioned me saying:

[Master Yun Gu]: The reason why mundane people are unable to attain sagehood is because they have too many wandering and false thoughts running through their minds. In our three-day meditation, I have not observed the slightest wandering thought arise in you—why is this so?

[Liao-Fan]: I replied, "Mr. Kong has clearly predicted the entire outcome of my life. I have seen that the time of life, death, promotion, and failure are all predestined. There is no use or need for me to think about it or to desire anything. That's why you have not seen me give rise to a single wandering thought." Master Yun Gu laughed and said:

[Master Yun Gu]: I thought you were someone of remarkable capabilities! Now I realize you are nothing but a common mundane person!

[Liao-Fan]: Feeling confused by what he said, I asked the Master to explain. He answered:

[Master Yun Gu]: An average person's mind is forever occupied by his wandering and imaginary thoughts, so naturally their lives are bound by the chi of ying-yang and fate. We cannot deny the fact that fate exists, but only ordinary people are bound by it. Fate cannot bind those who cultivate great kindness,

[Narrator]: Because their virtues accrued

from kind acts are so great that these acts will alter their 'original' destiny for the better.

[Master Yun Gu]: The merits accrued can actually change their destiny from suffering to happiness, poverty to prosperity, and short lives to longevity. Similarly, fate cannot bind those who commit great evils.

[Narrator]: When a person's evil deeds are so great and powerful, they will cancel out the fortune and prosperity predetermined in his original fate, and his life can be transformed from good to bad.

[Master Yun Gu]: For the past twenty years, you have lived your life according to Mr. Kong's predictions and did not do a thing to change it. Instead, you became bound by your own fate. If you're not considered as a mundane mortal, then who is?

[Liao-Fan]: Taken aback, I proceeded to ask Master Yun Gu, "According to you then, is it true that one can change one's fate, that one can escape from it?" The Master answered:

11

[Master Yun Gu]: Fate is created by ourselves. Good fortune or bad fortune are also determined by ourselves. When I commit evil, disasters are bound to strike. When I cultivate kindness, good fortune will naturally come my way. It says so in all the great ancient books of wisdom. In the Buddhist teachings, it is written that if one wishes and seeks wealth, position, a son, a daughter, or longevity, one can attain them. One only has to cultivate kind deeds in order to escape the control of fate. Since untruthful speech is one of the greatest offenses in Buddhist teachings, we can be assured that these are not lies. Buddhas and Bodhisattvas certainly have no reasons to deceive us.

[Liao-Fan]: I did not quite understand what he meant by 'attaining all that one wished for', and so I asked him, "Mencius once said,

[Mencius]: 'Whatever is sought for can be attained. The seeking is in oneself.'

[Liao-Fan]: This refers to inner qualities such as virtue, kindness, and morality. These are all qualities one can work

12

towards. However, when it comes to outside factors such as wealth, fame, and prestige, how can we seek and attain them? Don't these have to be granted by others in order to be achieved? The Master replied:

[Master Yun Gu]: Mencius was correct, but you misinterpreted his meaning. Hui-Neng, the Sixth Patriarch of the Zen school has taught that:

[Hui-Neng]: All the fields of merit are within one's own heart. If one seeks from within, one can be in touch with all fortunes and disasters. The outside is merely a reflection of the inside.

[Master Yun Gu]: By seeking within ourselves, we can not only attain the inner qualities of virtue, kindness, and morality, but we can also attain wealth, fame, and prestige.

[Narrator]: If wealth, fame, and prestige are embodied in one's fate, then one will attain them even without having to seek. If they are not, then one cannot attain them even through plotting and scheming.

[Master Yun Gu]: Therefore, if one cannot reflect within his own heart but instead blindly seeks fame, fortune, and longevity from external sources, then this seeking will be in vain. Just as Mencius once said:

[Mencius]: 'In seeking, one should follow the right path. In attaining, one attains what one's destiny entitles him to.'

[Narrator]: Whatever is attained in the end is still part of one's own fate.

[Master Yun Gu]: If one tries to seek these qualities from the outside, and even goes to the extent of committing evil deeds for them, then one will not only lose one's inner qualities of virtue and kindness, but predetermined fortune as well. Furthermore, evils committed in one's greedy mind to obtain more will often reduce the fortune of one's original fate. From this we can see that no benefit is derived from blind seeking.

[Liao-Fan]: Master Yun Gu continued to ask:

[Master Yun Gu]: What were Mr. Kung's predictions regarding your entire life?

[Liao-Fan]: I told him in great detail, from the placement positions in the examinations, to my appointment as an official, and finally, the date of my death.

[Master Yun Gu]: Do you feel you deserve imperial appointments or a son?

[Liao-Fan]: I reflected upon my previous deeds and attitudes in the past for a long time. Then I answered him saying, "No, I do not feel I deserve an imperial appointment or a son. Those who receive imperial appointments all have the appearance of good fortune, and I do not. I do not work towards accumulating virtues to build up my fortune, either. I am very impatient, intolerant, undisciplined, and speak without any restraint. I also have a strong sense of pride and arrogance. These are all signs of scant fortune and non-virtue, How is it possible for me to receive an imperial appointment?

[Narrator]: Next we will see why Liao-Fan has no children. Liking cleanliness is a good thing, but it can become a personality problem if one gets too immaculate. There is an old saying, 'life springs from the

15

dirt of the earth, and water too clean often harbors no fish.'

[Liao-Fan]: The first reason why I feel I do not deserve a son is because I am addicted to cleanliness, resulting in the lack of thoughtfulness for others. The second reason is that:

[Narrator]: 'Harmony is the cultivator of all life'.

[Liao-Fan]: But I have a quick temper and easily become angry. The third reason is based on the principle that:

[Narrator]: 'Loving kindness is the basis of reproduction, and harshness is the root of sterility',

[Liao-Fan]: I overly guard my own reputation and cannot sacrifice anything for the sake of others. The fourth reason is that I talk too much which wastes a lot of *chi*, or energy. The fifth reason is that I also delight in drinking alcohol, and that depletes my spirit.

[Narrator]: To remain healthy, one must not

16

sleep during the daytime and stay up through the nights.

[Liao-Fan]: The sixth reason I do not have a son is my habit of staying up nights, not knowing how to conserve my energy. Aside from these, I have many, many, other faults which are too numerous to mention. Master Yun Gu then said:

[Master Yun Gu]: According to you then, there are too many things in life you do not deserve, not only fame and a son!

[Narrator]: We should know that both good and bad fortune are all formed from one's heart; a wise person knows that everything one achieves or fails at in life are only consequences of their own actions and thoughts. Only a fool assumes that all is the work of fate and destiny!

[Master Yun Gu]: We must understand that those who have thousands of dollars in this life must have cultivated the fortune worthy of that amount in the past. Those who have hundreds of dollars must also have fortune which is worthy of containing that sum. Those whose fate is to die of starvation, in fact were meant to die in that manner. We must understand that the fate of these people was created by their own past thoughts and actions; the retribution today is simply the fruit of their deeds. Heaven does nothing more than punish evil beings with the suffering they deserve, and reward kind ones with the fortune they deserve.

[Narrator]: The following section is Master Yun Gu's advice to Liao-Fan, using the views of worldly folk, persuading him to cultivate virtue.

[Master Yun Gu]: Bearing children is similar to bearing fruit from seeds; if the seeds are planted well, so will the fruits they bear. If the seeds are not planted well, then the fruits will become malnourished. For example, if a person has accumulated enough merit and virtue for a hundred generations, then he or she will have descendants to last a hundred generations. One who accumulates enough merit and virtue to last ten generations will then have ten generations of descendants to live out that fortune. The same goes for three generations or two generations. For those who have no descendants at all, it is because they have not accumulated enough good merit and virtue – they may have amassed sins instead!

[Master Yun Gu]: Now that you recognize your own shortcomings, you can work to change and reform the misdeeds which cause you to not have a son or become an imperial official. You must cultivate virtue, tolerance, and treat others with compassion and harmony. You must also care for your health and conserve your energy and spirit. Live as though everything of the past dissolved yesterday, and all of the future begins today. If you can accomplish this, then you are a person born anew. If even our physical body is governed by the law of fate, then how can a mind of virtue and discipline not evoke a response from heaven? As said in the Tai Ja Chapter in the Chinese Book of History,

[Narrator]: 'One may run from the decrees of heaven, but one can never escape the retribution for one's own evil deeds'. In other words, one can alter the retribution

due from past deeds, but if one continues
to behave immorally, then there is no chance
of avoiding disaster.

[**Master Yun Gu**]: It is also said in the <u>Book
of Poems</u>,

[**Narrator**]: 'A person should often reflect
upon his own thoughts and actions, to see
if they accord with the ways of heaven. If
one practices such, then fortune will come
without being sought. The choice to seek
either good fortune or to bring about
adversity is all up to you.'

[**Master Yun Gu**]: Mr. Kong had predicted
that you will not receive an imperial
appointment or have a son. We can think of
these as the decrees of heaven, but even
that can still be changed. You only need to
reform your ill ways, practice kind deeds
and work to accumulate merit and virtue.
These are your own transactions to create
fortune, no one can take it away. How is it
then possible that you will not get to enjoy
it?

[**Narrator**]: The <u>I Ching</u>, <u>Book of Change,</u>
was written to help kind people bring about

good fortune and avoid adversity.

[Master Yun Gu]: If everything is predestined with no room for change, how can we improve upon our fortune and avoid adversity? The very first chapter of I Ching also said;

[Narrator]: 'Families who often perform kind deeds will have an excess of good fortune to pass onto the next generations.

[Master Yun Gu]: Do you believe in this?

[Liao-Fan]: I understood and believed in the Master, and paid my respects to him in gratitude. Then I began to repent of all my past wrongdoings, whether large or small, in front of the Buddha image. I wrote down my wish to pass the imperial examinations, and vowed to complete three thousand meritorious deeds to show my gratitude towards heaven, earth, and ancestors. Upon hearing my vow, Master Yun Gu showed me a chart, and taught me how to keep a daily record of the kind and evil acts I committed. He told me that bad deeds could neutralize the merits I accrue from good deeds. The Master also taught me how to recite the *Jwun*

Ti Mantra; it is a way to train my mind for single-minded concentration. Only with a pure and unscattered mind could what I seek for come true. Master Yun Gu then said:

[Master Yun Gu]: You can also learn the proper way to practice the art of written mantras. It is said, "Those who practice the art but do not know the right way to do it will be laughed at by gods and spirits." The secret behind writing mantras is the absence of thought from start to finish. In the process of drawing, one must not give rise to a single improper thought; even kind thoughts have to be let go of. Only under these circumstances can a mantra be successful. When one prays or seeks something in terms of changing fate, it is important that one does it when the mind is still. In this way, wishes will be easily fulfilled.

[Master Yun Gu]: Mencius stated in his Principle of Forming Destiny that:

[Mencius]: There is no difference between longevity and short life.

[Master Yun Gu]: At first glance, one would

find this hard to understand – how can longevity and short life be the same? In actuality, when we look within our hearts, we will find no duality, no difference. We should see everything with eyes of equality and live morally regardless of good or bad times. If one can practice accordingly, then one can master the fate of wealth and poverty.

[Master Yun Gu]: Therefore, when we are able to create and form our own destiny, it does not matter whether we are presently rich or poor.

[Narrator]: Just as a wealthy man should not become careless in his thoughts and actions because he is rich, a poor man should not resort to committing evil deeds due to his poverty. In either case, one should keep to one's place in society and be a virtuous person.

[Master Yun Gu]: If one can practice morality regardless of conditions, then he or she will surely change a poor life into a prosperous one, and a prosperous life into an even longer lasting prosperity.

[Master Yun Gu]: One should also look upon long life and short life equally. A person who knows he is short-lived should not think, 'I'm going to die soon anyway, so there's no point in being virtuous, I should steal and kill for my benefit while I can.'

[Narrator]: Instead, one who already knows he has a short life to live should be even more diligent in cultivating kindness, hoping to gain a longer life next time, and perhaps his or her merits from practicing kindness can even elongate the present life.

[Master Yun Gu]: One who is long-lived should not think, 'I have all the time in the world, it doesn't matter if I do some evil once in while.'

[Narrator]: We should know that longevity does not come easily, and should be cherished and used to cultivate even more kindness and virtue. Otherwise, you may very well use up your longevity all too soon.

[Master Yun Gu]: If you understand this

principle, then you will be able to change a short life into a long life through virtuous behavior.

[Master Yun Gu]: The issue of life and death is the most critical issue of one's life. Therefore, long life and short life is also the most important issue to us. The same applies to wealth and poverty, low and high prestige. These are all encompassed by the issue of long life and short life.

[Narrator]: That is why Mencius did not need to mention the latter in his principle of creating destiny, since he had already spoken about long and short life.

[Liao-Fan]: Master Yun Gu then told me about Mencius's teaching on cultivating the self. He said that:

[Master Yun Gu]: One who wishes to cultivate himself must do so day by day, and be mindful of his conduct every moment, ensuring that no transgressions are made. As for changing one's destiny, that depends on the accumulation of merit, seeking for a response from the heavens. When cultivating the self, one should be aware of one's own faults, and resolve to correct them just as in curing a sickness. Perseverance is required, and attainment comes when one's practice matures and ripens. In that case, one's destiny will most definitely change for the better. We should work toward severing all bad habits and thoughts. It would be quite an accomplishment for the true benefits of these teachings to be felt once you reach the state of 'no thought'.

[Master Yun Gu]: The actions of worldly people usually follow their thoughts. Whatever has to be 'thought' is not considered natural. I know that you are still unable to accomplish the state of 'no thought', but if you practice reciting the *Jwun Ti Mantra* continuously, it will help you to overcome scattered thoughts in the mind. When you recite, you must not think of reciting, but recite consciously and diligently without any attachment. When the reciting becomes second nature to you, it will be efficacious.

[Narrator]: But the essence of this

practice can only be understood after you practice it.

[Liao-Fan]: My name used to be Shuei Hai, which meant 'broad learning', but after receiving these teachings from Master Yun Gu, I changed it to Liao Fan, which means 'transcending the mundane'. It signified my understanding of the fact that destiny is created by ourselves, and I did not wish to be like worldly people, who allowed destiny to control them.

[Liao-Fan]: From then on, I began to be constantly aware of my thoughts and actions, and I was very cautious and careful in whatever I did. Soon I felt quite different from before. In the past, I used to be careless and lived my days in distraction, and had no self-discipline at all. Now, I found myself being naturally respectful, careful and conservative in my thoughts, speech, and actions. I maintain this attitude even when I'm alone, for I know that there are spirits and gods everywhere who can see my every action and thought. Even when I encounter people who dislike or slander me, I can take their insults with

27

a patient and peaceful mind, and not feel compelled to quarrel with them.

[Liao-Fan]: The year after I met Master Yun Gu, I took the preliminary imperial exam in which Mr. Kong had predicted I would come in third place. Amazingly, I came in first! Mr. Kong's predictions were beginning to lose their accuracy. He had not predicted I would pass the imperial exam at all, but that autumn, I did! None of these were part of my original destiny. Master Yun Gu had said that:

[Master Yun Gu]: Destiny could be changed.

[Liao-Fan]: And now I believe it more than ever!

[Liao-Fan]: Although I had corrected a lot of my faults, I found that I could not wholeheartedly do the things I ought to do. Even if I did do them, it was forced and unnatural. I reflected within and found that there were still many wrongs in my being,

[Narrator]: Such as seeing an opportunity

to practice kindness and not being eager enough to do it; or, harboring doubts when helping others in need.

[Liao-Fan]: Sometimes I forced myself to act kindly, but my speech was still untamed and offensive. I found I could contain myself when sober, but after a few drinks, I would lose self-discipline and act without restraint. Although I often practiced kind deeds and accumulated merits, my faults and offenses were so numerous, they seemed to outnumber my good deeds. A lot of my time was spent vainly and without value. It took me more than ten years to complete the three thousand meritorious deeds I had vowed to do.

[Liao-Fan]: I was not able to dedicate the merits from these three thousand kind deeds at a temple until I returned to my hometown in the south a few years later. Then I made my second wish, and that was for a son. I vowed to complete another three thousand good deeds. A few years later, your mother gave birth to you, and named you Tien-chi.

[Liao-Fan]: Every time I performed a kind

deed, I would record it in a book. Your
mother, who could not read or write, would
use a goose feather dipped in ink and make
a red circle on the calendar for every kind
deed she did. Sometimes she gave food to the
poor, or bought living creatures from the
marketplace to free in the wild.   She
recorded all of these with her circles on
the calendar. At times she could accumulate
more than ten red circles in one day!

[Narrator]: That means she performed more
than ten kind deeds in a single day.

[Liao-Fan]: Everyday we practiced like
this, and in four years, the three thousand
deeds were completed. Once again I made the
dedications, this time in our home. On
September 13th of that same year, I made my
third wish, and that was to pass the next
level in the imperial exam, the *jin-shr*
level. I also vowed to complete ten thousand
meritorious deeds. After three years, I
attained my wish and passed the *jin-shr*
level.   I was also made the mayor of Bao-di
prefecture. While in that office, I
prepared a small booklet to record my merits
and faults, and called it the Book of

Disciplining the Mind.

[Narrator]: The book was called Disciplining the Mind in hopes of helping him avoid selfish and improper thoughts.

[Liao-Fan]: From that day, I recorded all my good and bad deeds in that booklet, and kept it on my desk. Every evening, I would burn incense and make a report of my deeds to the heavens at the little altar in the garden. Once, your mother was concerned when she saw that I had not accumulated many merits and asked:

[Mother]: In the past, I was able to help you in your accumulation of kind deeds, and we were able to complete the three thousand meritorious deeds. Now, you have made a vow to complete ten thousand kind deeds, and there are fewer opportunities to practice them here at the government residence; how long will it be before your vow can be fulfilled?

[Liao-Fan]: That night, after your mother spoke these words, I dreamed of a heavenly being, and told him of my difficulty in completing the ten thousand kind deeds. The heavenly being said to me:

[Heavenly being]: When you became mayor, you reduced the taxes on the rice fields; that was a great kind deed, and that deed itself was worth ten thousand merits. Your vow is already fulfilled!

[Liao-Fan]: As it turned out, the farmers in Bao-di prefecture had to pay a very high tax, and when I came to office, I reduced the taxes on the rice fields by nearly half. But still, I felt strange...

[Narrator]: How did the heavenly being know about the tax deduction? Liao-Fan still held doubts and wondered how a single deed could be worth ten thousand merits.

[Liao-Fan]: Coincidentally, the Zen Master Huan-yu was traveling from the *Five Plateau Mountains* and stopped in Bao-di. I invited him over and told him of my dream, and asked whether it was believable. Master Huan-yu said:

[Master Huan-Yu]: When doing kind deeds,

one must be true and sincere, and not seek any rewards, or act with falsity. If one does a kind deed with such a true and sincere heart, then one deed can indeed be worth the merit from ten thousand kind deeds. Besides, your act of reducing the taxes in this prefecture benefits more than ten thousand people; you have relieved the suffering of heavy taxes on all these farmers. The fortune you will gain from this act will surely be great!

[Liao-Fan]: Upon hearing his words, I was overwhelmed with gratitude and immediately gave a month's salary for him to take back to the *Five-Plateau Mountains* as donation. I asked the Master to use the money to offer food for ten thousand monks and dedicate the merits for me.

[Liao-Fan]: Mr. Kong had predicted that I would die at the age of fifty-three. However, I survived that year with no illnesses though I did not ask the heavens for a longer life. Now I am sixty-nine, and I have lived sixteen more years than what was destined!

[Liao-Fan]: The Chinese <u>Book of History</u> had said:

[Narrator]: 'The way of the Heavens is undetermined, and neither is one's destiny.'

[Liao-Fan]: It is also said that,

[Narrator]: 'Destiny is not set, but is only created and determined by oneself.'

[Liao-Fan]: These are all true, and I have come to understand that both fortune and adversity are all results of one's own doings. These are truly the words of sages and saints! If one is to say that fortune and adversity are all determined by the heavens, then I would consider that person to be mundane and common.

[Liao-Fan]: Tien-Chi, my son, I wonder how your life will be? In any case of destiny, we should always prepare for the worst; therefore, even in times of prosperity, you must act as if you were not, and when things are going your way, you must be mindful of adversity. When you are wealthy, be mindful of poverty, and when loved and respected by all, you must remain careful and conservative. When the family is greatly respected and revered, you must carry yourself humbly, and when your learning is broad and deep, you must not display it, but keep it humbly within.

[Narrator]: The six ways of contemplation mentioned above are a means to tackle the problem from its opposite side. If one can thus cultivate the mind, then virtue and morality will grow and fortune will increase on its own.

[Liao-Fan]: When mindful of the past, we should spread the virtues of our ancestors, and when mindful of the present, we should conceal the faults of our own parents. This is what Mencius said as:

[Mencius]: 'Parents caring for children and children caring for parents'.

[Liao-Fan]: When mindful of the nation, we should think of how we can repay its kindness to us, and when mindful of the family, we should think of how to bring about good fortune. When mindful of the outside, we should think of how to help those in need around us, and when mindful of within, we should prevent wicked thoughts and improper actions from arising.

[Narrator]: These six contemplations are all positive ways to cultivate good character. If one can practice accordingly, one will surely become a true gentleman.

[Liao-Fan]: A person must be able to detect his faults everyday in order to correct them everyday. If you are unable to detect any faults in yourself, then improvement of character is out of the question. There are many intelligent people in the world who refuse to cultivate morality and virtue, and cannot put forth diligent effort in their work. Their failures later in life are owed to a single word: Laziness.

[Liao-Fan]: The teachings which Master Yun Gu taught are truly the most worthy, deep, real, and proper teachings, and I hope you will study them closely and practice them with all your effort. You must use your time wisely and not let it slip by in vain.

36

📖 The Second Lesson: Ways to Reform

[Narrator]: *How can we be free from faults when we were not born as saints or sages? Confucius once said, "One with faults should not fear to correct them." After Liao-fan spoke of the ways to create destiny, he proceeded to tell his son about the three ways to reform. First, one must feel shame, second one must know fear, and third, one must have determination and courage. If we are mindful of correcting even the tiniest mistake, then large wrongdoings would naturally be avoided.*

[Narrator]: The Spring-Autumn Period mentioned throughout this book refers to a period in China's history over 2,000 years ago when the country was undergoing great change and turmoil.

[Liao-Fan]: During the Spring-Autumn Period, China was divided into several small nations. Many prestigious advisors and counselors of these nations were able to accurately predict whether a person's future would be good, bad, disastrous or fortunate, based on their observation of that person's speech and behavior. These can all be seen recorded in several history books.

[Liao-Fan]: Usually, there are signs which signal impending danger or of coming good fortune. These signs are a reflection of one's heart; though it is the heart from which thoughts arise, the body and its limbs can fully portray a person's character.

[Narrator]: For instance, if a person is kind-hearted, then his every gesture would indicate steadiness and solidity. If a person is evil and mean, then his body and limbs would naturally portray a petty and small character.

[Liao-Fan]: Often a person is more fortunate when he tends toward kindness and invites trouble when he tends toward meanness.

[Liao-Fan]: Worldly people often do not see what is actually going on, as if their vision was blurred. Since they cannot see reality, they claim that fortune and disasters are unpredictable.

[Liao-Fan]: When a person is absolutely honest and truthful, his heart is in agreement with the heart of heaven. Therefore, when one can use this sincere attitude in treating people and dealing with everyday matters, good fortune will naturally follow. This means that in observing someone, we only need to pay attention to his behavior. If his behavior portrays kindness, then you will know for sure in advance that his good fortune is not far behind.

[Narrator]: On the contrary, when we see unkind behavior from a person, we will know that troubles await him. If you really want to have good fortune, and stay away from adversity, it is necessary to first reform your faults before practicing kind deeds.

[Liao-Fan]: There are three ways to reform one's faults: First, one must feel shame. Think of all the ancient saints and sages whose names and teachings have lasted through hundreds of generations. They were people just like us, but why is my name tarnished and my reputation ruined in just

39

one lifetime? I find that it is because I over-indulge myself in material pleasures and have been badly influenced by the polluted environment. I also secretly do many things I'm not supposed to do, and think others won't know about it. Sometimes I disregard the nation's laws and am not ashamed of it. Without realizing it, I stoop lower each day until I'm no different from an animal. There is nothing else in the world which calls for more shame and remorse than these behaviors. Mencius once said,

(Mencius): "Shame" is the greatest and most important word in a person's lifetime. Why? Because one who knows shame, will put forth his best effort in reforming faults and will eventually attain sagehood or become a saint. One who cannot comprehend the word 'shame' will be unrestrained and immoral. This person would then be just like an animal.

(Liao-Fan): These are really key words to reforming your faults.

(Liao-Fan): The second way to reform is

that one must know fear. What are we to fear? We must know that the heaven, earth, spirits, and gods all hover over our heads in observation.

[Narrator]: They are different from man in that they can see everything without obstruction. Therefore, it is not easy to deceive them.

[Liao-Fan]: Even when my wrongdoings are done in a place where nobody is around to witness it, the heaven, earth, spirits and gods are just like a mirror, clearly reflecting all my faults. If my offense is serious, then all kinds of disasters will befall me; if the fault is minor, it will still deduct from my current fortune. How can I not feel fear?

[Liao-Fan]: Every moment, even when I'm in an empty room, the spirits and gods watch over me very carefully and records everything. We can try covering up our evil doings from others,

[Narrator]: But the spirits and gods can see through to our hearts and know our every action.

(Liao-Fan): Ultimately, we cannot deceive ourselves. We would feel embarrassed and dishonored if others happened to see our misdeeds. Therefore, how can we not be constantly cautious of our every actions and be fearful of the consequences they might evoke?

(Liao-Fan): But there's more to it! As long as a person still has one breath left, then he has the chance to repent of the most serious mistakes and offenses.

(Narrator): Once, a person who behaved badly during his entire lifetime felt remorse just when he was about to die. He had realized his past mistakes and regretted all the bad things he had done. His heart came to a very kind thought, and immediately afterwards, he passed away peacefully.

(Liao-Fan): This is to say, if a person can have an overwhelming and courageous kind thought at the most important moment, then it can cleanse away hundreds of years of accumulated sins. This is just like how only one lamp is necessary to bring light into a valley that has been dark for a thousand years. Therefore, it does not matter how long one has been sinful, or if the offenses were newly made; he or she is a surpassing person as long as they are able to change!

[Narrator]: Though we make mistakes, it is good to correct them. But don't think it is all right for you to do bad things now because you can always repent later. This is definitely not allowed. If one commits a wrongdoing purposely, then the sin is even greater than before.

[Liao-Fan]: Besides, we are living in a tumultuous and constantly changing world. Our body, being made of flesh and blood is extremely perishable. If our next breath does not come, then this body will no longer be part of us. By then, even if we did want to reform, we would not have the chance to do so.

[Narrator]: Also, when a person dies, he cannot take any worldly possessions with him; for only his karma stays with his

43

spirit.

[Liao-Fan]: Therefore, when you commit evil, your retribution in the physical world is a bad reputation and name which will last for hundreds and thousands of years. Even filial children and loving grandchildren cannot cleanse your name for you. Whereas in your afterlife, you might end up in hell suffering immeasurable pain. Even the saints, sages, Buddhas, and Bodhisattvas you may meet cannot save or help you from your consequences. So how can one not be fearful?

[Liao-Fan]: The third way to reform is: one must have determination and courage.

[Narrator]: A person who hesitates to reform his faults is one who really does not want to change, but is content with what he can get away with.

[Liao-Fan]: His willpower may not be strong enough, making him afraid to change his wrongdoings. For a reform to take place, one must use all his efforts and resolve to change immediately. One should not doubt or wait to reform one's faults. We should not postpone our resolve to change until tomorrow or the day after. A minor fault is like a thorn sticking into our flesh, and should be quickly removed. A big fault is like a finger bitten by a poisonous snake. We must cut off that finger without hesitation to prevent the poison from spreading and taking our life.

[Liao-Fan]: If a person can follow the three ways of shame, fear, and determination to reform, then his personality will surely be transformed. Just as a thin layer of ice is melted by the sun's rays in springtime, one's faults will also disappear when dealt with through these three ways.

[Liao-Fan]: There are also three methods of practice in helping one reform. First is changing through action; second is changing through reasoning, and third is changing from the heart.

[Narrator]: Since the methods vary, so do the results of change. First let us talk about *changing through action*.

[Liao-Fan]: For example, if I killed living beings in the past, I now vow not to kill again starting today. If I was angry and yelled at others in the past, I vow not to get angry starting today. This is how a person changes through action, and refrains from repeating a wrongdoing by vowing not to do it again. However, it is a hundred times harder if you force yourself not to do something than if you just stopped doing it naturally. If you do not uproot your faults, but merely suppress them, the faults will eventually resurface even if you have temporarily stopped doing them. Therefore, the method of changing through action cannot help you get rid of your faults permanently.

[Liao-Fan]: Second, let me explain changing through reasoning. A person who tries to reform can refrain from wrongdoings by understanding the reason and principle behind why he should not do it. In the instance of killing, one can reform through contemplating:

[Narrator]: Loving all living things is the

virtue of heaven. All living beings love life and are afraid to die. How can I be at peace with myself by taking another's life to nurture my own? At times, animals were even cooked alive, such as fish or crabs. They may not have been completely slaughtered before going into the cooking pot. Such pain and suffering reach down into the bones, how can we be so cruel to these animals? When we eat, we use all kinds of expensive and tasty things to nourish our bodies, enough to fill the whole dinner table! But once the meal is done, even the delicacies become body waste and are excreted. The result of our killing accomplishes nothing. We can be nourished just as well by consuming vegetarian foods. Why let your stomach become a graveyard and reduce your fortune through the sin of killing?

(**Liao-Fan**): Think again of all the living beings with flesh and blood. Like us, they have a consciousness. We should cultivate virtue and allow these living beings to feel safe around us. How can we continue to harm their lives and make them hate us? If you think about it, you will naturally feel sorrow for these animals and be unable to swallow their flesh.

[Liao-Fan]: Here's another example of *change through reasoning*. One who often gets angry should stop and think of the fact that everyone has their individual strengths and weaknesses. According to my reasoning, if I touched on someone else's weakness, I should pity him for his weaknesses and forgive his shortcomings. If someone offends me for no reason at all, then it is their problem, and that has nothing to do with me. There is no reason for me to get angry. I can also think:

[Narrator]: There isn't a right minded person who thinks he is always right, for anyone who thinks he is perfect must be a fool. There isn't a learned person who blames another for being knowledgeable, because a truly learned person would be humble, and he will only criticize himself and treat others with tolerance. Therefore, one who complains about others is not a genuine learned person.

[Liao-Fan]: Therefore, when things do not

go the way we wish, it is because we haven't cultivated our virtues and morals, and have not accumulated enough merits to move others! We should always reflect upon ourselves first and see whether we have mistreated others.

(Narrator): If we practice thus and diligently cultivate this virtue, then adversity and slander can actually become our training ground to refine our character and to fulfill our goals.

(Liao-Fan): Therefore, we should be very glad to accept someone else's criticism and teachings. What is there to be angry and complain about?

(Liao-Fan): Additionally, to remain unmoved by slander is like letting a torch burn itself out in space. If we hear others slandering us and try to defend ourselves, it would be like the spring silkworm spinning its own cocoon. There was an old saying which stated:

(Narrator): 'One who ties himself in a cocoon is looking for suffering'.

[Liao-Fan]: Therefore, no benefit but harm is derived from getting angry. There are other faults and offenses we can change along the same lines. If we can understand the reasoning behind the need for reform, we will not make the same mistakes twice.

[Liao-Fan]: Lastly, what is meant by *changing from the heart*? Though a person's faults can amount to thousands of different types, they all stem from thoughts of the mind. If my heart is still of thoughts, then actions will not arise and faults can be avoided. If your heart is rooted in vices such as desire, fame, profits, or anger, you don't have to find ways to get rid of each fault. All you need is a sincere, kind heart and the willingness to practice kind deeds. As long as your heart is virtuous and kind, then naturally your mind will not generate any improper thoughts.

[Liao-Fan]: All mistakes stem from the heart; therefore, one should change from the heart. It is like getting rid of a poisonous tree. If you want to put an end to it, you must uproot it altogether so it cannot grow again. Why exert yourself to no avail by pulling out its leaves one by one and cutting it twig by twig?

(**Liao-Fan**): The best way to reform our faults is through cultivating our hearts. If we are willing to cultivate our hearts, then it is possible to purify our faults right away.

(**Narrator**): This is because wrongdoings originate from the heart.

(**Liao-Fan**): Purifying the heart can erase all improper and bad thoughts before they are carried out in action.

(**Liao-Fan**): If my heart is pure, I can recognize and stop an evil thought as soon as it arises. The immoral idea will disappear the moment I lay my conscious on it. If I am unable to succeed at reforming a fault through changing the heart, then I will try at the level of understanding, knowing the reasons why I need to make the change. If I cannot succeed with this, then I will try to reform by changing through action and force the thought to dissipate.

The best way is by cultivating the heart and understanding the reason behind the need to change. The alternative way is forcing ourselves not to commit the wrongdoing again. Sometimes all three methods have to be used to succeed at reforming a fault.

[Narrator]: Don't be a fool by dismissing the best way and preferring the alternative way.

[Liao-Fan]: But even when one vows to change, assistance is needed to truly reform. We will need constant reminders from true friends who are witnesses to our actions in everyday life. As for our good and bad thoughts, we can ask the spirits and gods to be our witness. I practice this by writing down all my faults and reporting them to the heavens, earth, spirits, and gods. You also need to repent sincerely and wholeheartedly from morning to evening without laxity. If one can sincerely repent from one to two weeks, then one to three months, continuing this way, then one will definitely attain results and benefits.

[Narrator]: What are the benefits of

repentance? For one, you may feel very much at ease, and your heart will feel light and generous. A dumb person may suddenly become wise, and one can maintain a clear and relaxed mind even in a disturbing and confusing environment. One would also feel a great knowledge for everything. One would be able to drive out all hatred upon seeing an enemy and keep a happy attitude. One may dream of spitting out black things, a sign of expelling improper thoughts and negative energy, leaving the heart much cleaner and purified. One may also dream of the ancient saints or sages who have come to promote and help them, or dream of flying in space without a care in the world. One may also dream of all kinds of colorful flags and ornately decorated canopies. These unusual phenomena are all indications of a successful reform and dissolving of past offenses.

[Liao-Fan]: However, one must not consider seeing these phenomena as a sign of perfection. Instead, one must resolve to further improve the self and put forth greater effort to reform.

[Liao-Fan]: During the Spring-Autumn period of China's history, there was a high senior government official in Wei, named Bwo-yu Chu. When he was twenty, he was already mindful of his past faults. He studied his mistakes and tried to correct them thoroughly. At the age of twenty-one, he felt he still had not completely corrected all his faults. When he was twenty-two, he felt as if twenty-one was spent dreamily, without practical improvement. Thus, year after year, he continued to correct his faults. When he reached fifty, Bwo-yu still felt that the past forty nine years were full of wrongdoings.

[Narrator]: This was how particular our ancestors were regarding the correction of faults!

[Liao-Fan]: We are all just common people and our mistakes are as numerous as the spines on a porcupine. Oftentimes when we look back, we do not even see our own faults. This is because we are careless, and do not know how to reflect on our own actions. It is as if a cataract is growing in our eye,

54

we become so blind we cannot even see that we're making mistakes everyday!

[Liao-Fan]: There are also indications when people have accumulated too many offenses and sins.

[Narrator]: For instance, one's heart may feel confused and oppressed, lacking energy and spirit. One becomes extremely forgetful, full of worries and feels embarrassed and depressed upon meeting a virtuous gentleman. One becomes displeased at hearing righteous reasoning and when showing kindness to others, is in turn treated with hostility. One will constantly have nightmares where everything is upside-down, and will talk incoherently and behave abnormally. These are the symptoms of those who have accumulated too many sins and offenses!

[Liao-Fan]: If you have any of the above symptoms, you should immediately gather your willpower and reform all faults. It is necessary to form a new life for yourself. I hope you will not delay!

📖 The Third Lesson:
The Way to Cultivate Kindness

[Narrator]: *The previous chapter spoke about the many ways to correct one's faults in this present life, naturally assuring that a good life will not become a bad one. However, we are still unable to transform a bad life into a good one. Though we may be good and virtuous in this life, we do not know if we committed offenses in past lives. The retribution for past deeds still has to be undergone. Therefore, in order to change a bad life into a good life, we not only have to reform our faults, but also have to practice all forms of kindness and build upon our virtue. Only in this way can we rid ourselves of the karma created in the past. Once the number of our kind practices accumulate, our bad life will naturally turn into a good life; thus, the practice of changing destiny can be proven!*

[Liao-Fan]: The <u>I Ching/Book of Change</u> stated:

[Narrator]: "Families who perform kind deeds will accumulate fortune which can outlast many generations".

[Liao-Fan]: Let me give you an example. Once there was a family by the name of Yen. Before they agreed to give their daughter in marriage to the man who later became Confucius' father, they looked into the past deeds of the family. After finding the family to be one that practiced kindness and accumulated virtues, the Yen family felt assured that their daughter would be marrying into a family that would be prosperous with outstanding descendants. Sure enough, their daughter later gave birth to Confucius.

[Liao-Fan]: Confucius had once praised Shwun, an emperor of early China, on his filial piety, saying:

[Confucius]: Due to his great filial piety, Shwun and his ancestors will be known and respected by others. His offspring will be prominent for many, many generations.

[Liao-Fan]: These sayings were later proven true through history. Now I will prove to you in these true stories that merits can be attained through performing kind deeds.

[Liao-Fan]: In <u>Fukien</u> Province, there was a prominent man named Rong Yang who held a position in the imperial court as the Emperor's teacher. His ancestors were boat people who made a living by helping people cross the river. Once, there was a storm which lasted so long that fierce flooding washed away all the people's houses. People, animals, and goods were carried down river by the current. Other boaters took advantage of the situation and strove to collect the floating goods. Only Rong Yang's grandfather and great grandfather took interest in rescuing the drowning people. They did not take any of the goods that floated by. The other boaters all laughed and thought them to be very stupid. Later on, when Rong Yang's father was born, the Yang family gradually became wealthy. One day a saint disguised as a Taoist monk came to the Yang family and said:

[Taoist]: Your ancestors have accumulated a lot of merit; your offspring should enjoy wealth and prominence. There is a special place where you can build your ancestral tomb.

[Liao-Fan]: So they followed the Taoist's suggestion and shortly after, Rong Yang was born. Rong Yang passed the imperial examination when he was only twenty years old and later received imperial appointments.

[Narrator]: The emperor had even bestowed his grandfather and great grandfather with the same imperial honors. His descendants are still very prominent today.

[Liao-Fan]: Zi-cheng Yang from the prefecture of Ninpo, Chehkiang Province is another example. Zi-cheng worked as a member in the staff of the prefectural courthouse. He was a kind, humane, and law-abiding man. Once, the prefectural magistrate punished a criminal by beating him until his blood spilled out onto the ground. The magistrate's anger did not subside and as he was about to continue, Zi-cheng knelt and pleaded with him to stop beating the prisoner. The magistrate said:

[Magistrate]: It's all right for you to plead, but how can I not be angry when this person has broken the law!

59

[Liao-Fan]: Zi-cheng replied:

[Zi-cheng]: When even those in government positions of prestige and power are corrupted and do not follow the Righteous Path, how can one expect the common people to abide by laws and orders? Also, extreme beating can force an innocent suspect to plead guilty. Thus in a case like this we should be more understanding.

[Liao-Fan]: The magistrate was quite touched by Zi-cheng's speech and ceased the beating. Although Zi-cheng came from a very poor family, he never took any bribes. If the prisoners were short of food, he would always take food from his own home even if it meant going hungry himself. This practice of compassion never ceased and eventually Zi-cheng had two sons.

[Narrator]: The elder's name was Shou-chen and the younger was named Shou-zi. Both sons became very prominent, and held important government positions. Even the descendants of the Yang family remained prominent for a long time as well.

[Liao-Fan]: Here is another true story that happened during the Ming Dynasty. Once, an organization of bandits appeared in <u>Fukien</u> Province. The Emperor appointed General Hsieh to lead the imperial army to pacify them. General Hsieh wanted to make sure that the innocent were not accidentally killed in the hunt for bandits. So, he managed to attain a list of those who belonged to the organization and commanded that a white flag be given secretly to those who did not belong with the bandits. They were told to place the flag on their door when the imperial army came to town and the soldiers were ordered not to harm the innocent. With this one thought of kindness, General Hsieh saved tens of thousands of people from being killed.

[Narrator]: Later, his son Chian Hsieh placed first on the imperial exams and later became an advisor to the emperor. His grandson Pei Hsieh also placed highly on the exams.

[Liao-Fan]: Another example is the Lin family from <u>Fukien</u>. Among their ancestors was an old lady who was very generous. Everyday she made rice balls to give to the poor, and always gave as many as they asked for. There was a Taoist monk who came everyday for three years and each time would ask for six or seven rice balls. The old lady always granted his request and never expressed any displeasure. The Taoist monk, who was actually a heavenly being who came to test the depth of her kind heart, realized the deep sincerity of this woman's kindness and said:

[Taoist]: I have eaten your rice balls for three years with nothing to show my gratitude in return. Perhaps I can help you in this way: On the land behind your house there is a good place where you can build the ancestral grave. If you are placed there in the future, the number of your descendants who will have imperial appointments will be equivalent to the number of seeds in a pound of sesame seeds.

[Liao-Fan]: When the old lady passed away, the Lin family followed the Taoist's suggestion and buried her at the designated place. The first generation after that, nine men passed the imperial exams, and it continued that way for every succeeding generation.

(Liao-Fan): Another example comes from the father of an imperial historian whose name was Chi Feng. One winter many years ago, Chi Feng's father was on his way to school when he encountered a person frozen in the snow. Finding the man still breathing, he quickly took off his coat to wrap around the frozen man. He carried him back home and revived him. That night he dreamed of a heavenly being who told him:

(Heavenly being): You helped the dying man out of utter sincerity, this is a great virtue. I will bring the famous General Han-chi of the Sung Dynasty to be reborn as your son.

(Liao-Fan): Later the child was born and his nickname was Chi.

(Liao-Fan): Another example is of Ta-jo Ying, the imperial secretary who lived in Tai-chou. When he was young, he used to study in remote mountain areas. At night he often heard the sounds of ghost and spirits but he never feared them. One day he heard a ghost say happily to another ghost:

[Ghost 1]: There's a village woman whose husband left home a long time ago and has not returned. Her in-laws think that their son is dead and are forcing her to remarry. Tomorrow night she is going to commit suicide here, and will replace me so that I can be reborn.

[Narrator]: The souls of those who commit suicide have to wait for another to die at the same place they did in order to leave the ghost realm and attain rebirth at a higher level.

[Liao-Fan]: Mr. Ying heard this and immediately set out to sell his parcel of land. He attained four lians of silver and made up a letter from the daughter-in-law's husband and sent it to her home along with the silver. The father-in-law noticed that the letter was not in his son's handwriting, but examined the silver and said:

[Father-in-law]: The letter may be a fake,

but the sliver's not. Besides, who would send us this much money? Perhaps our son is truly alive and well, and we should not force our daughter-in-law to remarry.

[Liao-Fan]: Therefore the daughter-in-law did not commit suicide and her husband returned home after all. Mr.Ying heard the ghosts converse again:

[Ghost 1]: Humph! Originally I was able to leave this place for rebirth, but my chance got messed up by Mr. Ying!

[Ghost 2]: Why don't you inflict some harm on him?

[Ghost 1]: No, I can't. His goodness and virtue has been recognized by the gods and he's going to receive a prominent position in the future. How can I harm him'?

[Liao-Fan]: Mr. Ying heard this and became even more diligent in practicing kindness and accumulating merit. Whenever there was a famine, he would use his own money to buy food for the poor and needy and was always eager to help those in emergencies. When

65

things did not go his way, he always reflected within himself rather than complain of the outside conditions. Even today, his descendants are still very prominent.

[Liao-Fan]: There was another person, Feng-chu Hsu, who lived in Changso, <u>Chiangsu</u> Province, whose father was very wealthy. Whenever there was a famine, his father would donate his own grain and all the rent on the rice fields to the poor. One night he heard ghosts singing outside his home:

[Ghosts]: No kidding! No kidding! A person of the Hsu family is going to pass the imperial exam!

[Liao-Fan]: This went on for several days and sure enough, that year his son Feng-chu passed the imperial exam. From then on, he was even more diligent in doing good deeds and accumulating merit. He often fixed bridges and took care of travelers and monks. One day he heard the ghosts sing again:

[Ghosts]: No kidding! No kidding! A person in the Hsu family is going to pass an even higher level on the imperial exam!

[Narrator]: And sure enough, Feng-chu passed the higher exam and became the governor of two provinces.

[Liao-Fan]: Another example is Kung-hsi Tu who lived in Chia-shing, Chehkiang Province. Mr. Tu used to work in the courthouse and would spend nights in the prison cells, talking with the inmates. Whenever he found anyone to be innocent, he would write a classified report to the judge, informing him of innocent cases. The judge would then question the prisoners accordingly and clear the case.

[Narrator]: Through Mr. Tu's effort, ten innocent people were released, and all of them were extremely grateful to him. Soon after, Mr. Tu also made a report to the Imperial Judge saying:

[Mr. Tu]: If even in the Imperial City there are so many innocent imprisoned, there must be many more throughout the nation. I recommend that the Imperial Judge send investigators to check the prisons for innocent people every five years. The sentences can be reduced or canceled in order to prevent the innocent from remaining in prison.

(Liao-Fan): The Imperial Judge took his request to the Emperor, who agreed to Mr. Tu's suggestion. Mr. Tu was chosen as one of the special agents in charge of reducing sentences for those who may be innocent. One night he dreamed of a heavenly being who came to him and said:

(Heavenly being): You were not supposed to deserve a son in this life, but this act of reducing prison sentences for innocent people is in line with the wishes of the heavens. You will be bestowed with three sons and they will all attain high positions.

(Liao-Fan): Soon after that, his wife gave birth to three sons who all became prominent men in society.

(Liao-Fan): Another example of attaining

good outcomes from practicing kindness is Ping Bao who lived in Chia-shing. Ping was the youngest of the seven sons of the magistrate of Chih-chou, <u>An-hui</u> Province. He was sought into marriage by the Yuan family at Ping-hu Prefecture and was a good friend of my father. Ping Bao was very knowledgeable and talented, but he was never able to pass the exams.

[Narrator]: He put his time into studying the teachings of Buddhism and Taoism instead.

[Liao-Fan]: Once, while traveling to Lake Liu, he came to a village and saw a temple in desperate need of repairs. He saw that the statue of Kuan Yin Bodhisattva stood wet from the rain which leaked through the roof. Ping took out all his money and gave it to the abbot of the temple, asking him to please use it to restore the temple. The abbot replied:

[Abbot]: It will be a very big project, I'm afraid this amount is not enough to complete your wish.

[Liao-Fan]: Ping Bao then took out all his luxurious belongings and handed them to the abbot. His servant tried to persuade him into keeping his best outfit, but he refused, saying:

[Ping Bao]: It does not matter to me. As long as the statue of Kuan Yin Bodhisattva remains undamaged, I do not care if I have to go without clothes.

[Liao-Fan]: The abbot, with tears in his eyes, exclaimed:

[Abbot]: To give up money and clothing is not a difficult deed to accomplish, but your deep sincerity is truly rare and precious to encounter!

[Liao-Fan]: After the temple was repaired, Ping Bao led his father over to visit and spent the night there as well. That night, Ping dreamed of the Dharma Protector of the temple, Chle-lan, coming to thank him saying:

[Chie-Lan]: Since you have accumulated these merits and virtues, your children and descendants will enjoy having imperial appointments for a long time.

[Liao-Fan]: Later on, his son and grandson both passed high exams and were appointed as imperial officials.

[Liao-Fan]: Another example is a person named Li Zhi from Jia-shan prefecture. His father used to be a clerk in the prefectural courthouse. Once, Li's father came to know about an innocent man who was given the death penalty. He attempted to plead this case with his superior. When the prisoner heard about this, he told his wife:

[Prisoner]: I am so indebted to this man who has spoken on my behalf, and I have no way of showing my gratitude. Will you invite him over to our house and offer yourself in marriage? Perhaps this will please him and increase my chances to live.

[Liao-Fan]: The wife cried as she listened to his request, for she really did not want to do it. But it was the only way she could help her husband in this time of need. So, the next day when the clerk came to visit, she offered him wine and told him of her husband's wishes. The clerk refused the offer of marriage, but continued with great effort to clear the case. When at last the prisoner was released, he and his wife both went to his house to thank him. The man said:

(Man): One with such virtue as yours is truly rare to encounter these days, how can I show my gratitude? You do not have a son, please allow me to offer my daughter in marriage to you, this is the only way I can repay you. Please accept.

(Liao-Fan): So the clerk accepted, and soon afterwards, she bore him his son, Li Zhi. Li passed the higher level imperial exam when he was just twenty years old.

(Narrator): Li's son Gao, and grandson, Lu, and great grandson Da-lwun all passed high examinations and received imperial appointments.

(Liao-Fan): The ten examples above all tell of the different deeds cultivated by different people. Although their actions differ, their intent was the same: to do good. If we were to examine goodness closely, we would find that there are many different kinds.

[**Narrator**]: There is real goodness and false goodness, honest goodness and crooked goodness, hidden goodness and visible goodness, seeming goodness and unseeming goodness, improper goodness and proper goodness, half goodness and full goodness, big goodness and small goodness, and finally, difficult goodness and easy goodness.

[**Liao-Fan**]: These different types of goodness each have their own reason, which should be carefully learned and understood. If we practice kind deeds but do not learn the way to differentiate between right and wrong, we may end up doing harm instead of good. Now I will explain the different types of goodness one by one.

[**Liao-Fan**]: What is real goodness and false goodness? Once upon a time in the Yuan Dynasty, a group of scholars went to pay homage to Master Jung Feng on Tianmu Mountain. They asked:

[Scholar 1]: Buddhist teachings often speak of the retributions for good and evil; they say it's like the shadow, following the body wherever it goes.

[Narrator]: This is saying that doing good will always have its reward, and doing evil will always have its punishments.

[Scholar 1]: Then why is it, that there are people who practice kind deeds, but their family and descendants are not prosperous and successful? On the other hand, there are evil and wicked people who do bad things, but their family and descendants do quite well. Where has the law of cause and effect gone to? Is there no standard in the Buddha's teaching?

[Liao-Fan]: Master Jung Feng answered him, saying:

[Master J.F.]: Common people are blinded by worldly views, they have not cleansed their minds of impurities, and cannot see with true perception. Therefore, they look upon true goodness as evil and mistaken true evil as goodness. This is very common nowadays! Furthermore, these people do not blame themselves for bad perception on their part, but instead blame the heavens for their misfortunes!

[Scholar 2]: Goodness is goodness, and evil is evil; how can they be mistaken for each other?

[Liao-Fan]: Hearing this, Master Jung Feng asked each of them to express their thoughts on what was good and what was evil. One of them said:

[Scholar 3]: To yell at and beat others is evil, to respect and treat others in a mannerly way is good.

[Liao-Fan]: Master Jung Feng answered:

[Master J.F.]: Not necessarily.

[Liao-Fan]: Another scholar said:

[Scholar 4]: Being greedy for wealth and taking another's money is evil, not being greedy and abiding by proper ways is good.

75

[Liao-Fan]: Master Jung Feng said:

[Master J.F]: Not necessarily.

[Liao-Fan]: The remaining scholars all expressed their own views on what was good and what was evil, but Master Jung Feng still replied:

[Master J.F.]: Not necessarily.

[Liao-Fan]: Since Master Jung Feng disagreed with all of their views on good and evil, they decided to ask the Master himself. They questioned:

[Scholar 1]: So what is really considered good, and what is really considered evil?

[Liao-Fan]: Master Jung Feng told them:

[Master J.F.]: To do things with the intention of bringing benefit to others is good, to do things for the sake of oneself is evil. If what you do is for the sake of benefiting another, then it does not matter if you yell at or beat him, that is still

76

considered good. If your intention is for self-benefit, then regardless of your appearance of respect and courtesy, it is still considered evil. Therefore, when one practices kind deeds with the sole intention of benefiting others, this is considered as benefiting the public, and if it's public, then it is real goodness. If you only think for yourself while doing kind acts, then that is considered private benefit, and that, is false goodness. When kindness springs from within the heart, it is real goodness. When one does good just for the sake of doing a good deed, then it is false. Also, when one does good without expecting anything in return, it is considered real goodness. When one practices kind deeds for some other purpose than to benefit others, it is false. These differences should all be scrutinized by those who wish to practice true kindness.

[Liao-Fan]: What is honest goodness and crooked goodness? People nowadays often look upon a conservative and nice person as a good and kind person. However, the ancient sages and saints have shown that they prefer those who are courageous and hold high goals for themselves.

[Narrator]: This is because those with courage and high goals are easier to teach and guide, and will someday reach accomplishment in life, while those who are overly careful and conservative will never amount to anything.

[Liao-Fan]: As for those who appear to be conservative and careful in their everyday actions, they may be liked by all, but because of their weak personality, they easily go along with everything, unable to think for themselves. Sages often speak of them as thieves of virtue. From this we can see that the viewpoint of common folk greatly differs from that of the saints and sages.

[Narrator]: What common people may view as goodness, the saint in fact proclaims to be evil. What appears to be evil to the common people, the saint perceives as true kindness.

[Liao-Fan]: This applies to other matters as well. Heaven, earth, gods and spirits all look upon good and evil from the same viewpoint as the sages. The kind man finds himself rewarded for his kind deeds, and the wicked man suffers for his evil-doings. Whatever the sages perceive as right, they too see the same way. They do not view things from the same perspective as do commoners. Therefore, those who wish to accumulate merit must not be deceived and affected by the sights and sounds of the world, and should practice with a true and humble heart, not for the purpose of pleasing others and acquiring respect. One must protect one's heart from deviant and impure thoughts.

[Narrator]: Honest goodness comes from the thought to help all others, and crooked goodness arises from the thought of greed in wishing only to please people. In harboring love for others, this is being honest, and in harboring thoughts of hatred and jealousy, this is being crooked. Honest goodness is when one is respectful, and crookedness is when one acts without sincerity.

[Liao-Fan]: These should all be carefully

differentiated.

(Liao-Fan): What is hidden goodness and visible goodness?

(Narrator): When one does something good and people know about it, it is called visible goodness. When one does something good and no one knows about it, it is called hidden virtue.

(Liao-Fan): Those with hidden virtues will naturally be known by the heavens and will be rewarded. Those who practice visible goodness are known by people, and they enjoy fame.

(Narrator): Fame itself is a fortune, but fame is not favored by heaven and earth, for heaven and earth do not like those who seek fame.

(Liao-Fan): We can see that those who have great fame but lack the virtues supporting it will eventually encounter some kind of unthinkable adversity. A person who truly has not done any wrong but continues to be falsely accused by others will have descendants who will suddenly become prosperous and successful.

(Narrator): From this, we can see how important it is to know the minute differences between hidden and visible goodness. We cannot afford to mistake them!

(Liao-Fan): In performing good deeds, there is also what seems to be goodness but is actually not, and what does not appear to be goodness but actually is. For example, in the Spring-Autumn Period, there was a country named Lu. Because there were other countries which took their citizens as slaves or servants, the country of Lu made a law which rewarded those who paid the ransom to regain the freedom of their fellow citizens. At that time, Confucius had a very rich student named Dz-gong. Although Dz-gong paid for the ransom to free his people, he did not accept the reward for doing such a deed.

(Narrator): He did it out of good intention, seeking only to help others and not for the reward money.

[Liao-Fan]: But when Confucius heard this, he was very unhappy and scolded him saying:

[Confucius]: You acted wrongly in this matter. When saints and sages undertake anything, they strive to improve the social demeanor, teaching the common folk to be good and decent people. One should not do something just because one feels like it. In the country of Lu, the poor outnumber the wealthy. By refusing the reward, you lead others to think that accepting the reward money is being greedy, thus, all the poor people and others who do not wish to appear greedy will hesitate to pay for ransom in the future. Only very rich people will have a chance to practice this deed. If this happens, no one will pay the ransom to free our people again.

[Liao-Fan]: Another student of Confucius, Dz-lu, once saw a man drowning in the river, and went forth to rescue him. Later, the man thanked him by giving him a cow as a token of gratitude. Dz-lu accepted his gift. Confucius was happy when he heard this, and said:

[Confucius]: In the future, people will be willing and eager to help those who are drowning in deep waters or lakes.

[Liao-Fan]: If we look from the view of common people, Dz-gong, who did not accept the reward money, was good; and Dz-lu, who accepted the cow was not as good. Who would have known that Confucius praised Dz-lu instead and scolded Dz-gong? From this we can see that those who practice kind deeds must not only look at the present outcome,

[Narrator]: But should also consider the act's effect in the long run.

[Liao-Fan]: One should not only consider one's own gain and loss,

[Narrator]: But should look to see the impact made on the public.

[Liao-Fan]: What we do right now may be good,

[Narrator]: But with passing years it may inflict harm upon others.

[Liao-Fan]: Therefore, what seems like goodness may in fact be the opposite, and what appears to be the opposite of goodness, may someday turn out to be goodness done after all.

[Liao-Fan]: There are other examples of what appears to be goodness but actually is not. For example:

[Narrator]: There are many things that people ought to do, but sometimes these things prove to be better left undone. Forgiveness is a virtue, but it cannot be used without reason and wisdom. If we easily forgive and release a criminal when he has not repented and reformed, we may be letting loose a threat to society, causing more harm than good. In this case, forgiveness would be improper, and the man would be best left in his cell.

[Liao-Fan]: Everyone ought to have manners, but they should be carried out with good measure. Overdoing your courtesy to others can result in making them proud and arrogant. In this case, it would not be a good thing.

[Narrator]: Keeping to one's word is a virtue, but if one causes bigger trouble through keeping a small promise, then that would be considered improper also.

[Liao-Fan]: Being loving and compassionate is a wonderful trait, but if compassion is carried out by allowing anything to be done, then the spoiled person would be daring and unrestrained, causing greater harm and trouble in the future. This would be most unmerciful.

[Narrator]: These are all examples of what appears to be goodness but actually is not, and should be thoroughly contemplated.

[Liao-Fan]: What is improper goodness and proper goodness? In the Ming Dynasty, there once was a prime minister named Wen-yi Lyu, who was a just and lawful man. When he grew old, he retired to his hometown where he was loved and respected by all the people. Once, a drunken villager went to his home and proceeded to insult him. Mr. Lyu was not angered by his words but instead told his servant:

[Mr. Lyu]: This man is drunk; let's not give him a hard time.

[Liao-Fan]: With this, he closed the door and ignored the onslaught of insults. A year later, the same man committed a grave crime and was sent to jail with the death sentence. Upon hearing this, Mr. Lyu said with great remorse:

[Mr. Lyu]: If I had taken him to the authorities for punishment that day when he came to insult me, perhaps this would not have happened. A little discipline then could have prevented the great harm done now, and might have saved him from certain death. At that time, I was only thinking of being kind, and unknowingly nurtured a daring and outrageous character. Since nothing came from his deed of insulting a prime minister, he grew bold and went on committing the crimes which later brought him the death penalty.

[Liao-Fan]: This is an example of doing something bad while having good intentions.

[Liao-Fan]: There is also an example of

those who did good when they in fact intended otherwise. Once, a famine ravished the land, and people stole food from others in broad daylight. A rich family reported their stolen losses from the marketplace to the authorities, but the government did not want to get involved, and did nothing to stop the people. Eventually, the people grew more daring and chaos was imminent. So, the rich family took the law into their own hands and proceeded to catch and punish those who stole from them. In this way, peace returned to the land and the people stole no more from one another. It was with selfish intentions that the rich family acted, but the result of their deeds actually did everyone a great benefit.

[Narrator]: Therefore, we all know that goodness is proper, and evil is improper; but remember that there are cases where deeds done out of good intention resulted in evil, and deeds done with evil intentions resulted in good. This is saying that although the intention was proper, it resulted in the improper, and can only be said as the 'improper within the proper'. However, there is also the case when the improper was intended but resulted in the proper. This is called the 'proper within the improper'.

[Liao-Fan]: Everyone ought to know and understand this.

[Liao-Fan]: What is half goodness and full goodness? In the I Ching, Book of Change it is said:

[Narrator]: When a person does not accumulate kind deeds, he or she will not attain good fortune. When one does not accumulate evil deeds, he or she will not bring about great adversity.

[Liao-Fan]: The accumulation of kind and evil deeds greatly determines our future. If we are diligent in doing kind deeds, it is like collecting things in a container, and with diligence, it will soon be full, and we will have our reward of good fortune. If we are eager in the accumulation of evil deeds and gather that with great diligence, then the container of evil will soon be full and disasters will surely befall. If we are somewhat lazy in our collecting, either in kindness or evil, then the container will be left half filled, and neither good fortune nor adversity will come swiftly. This is one explanation of half goodness and full goodness.

[Liao-Fan]: Once there was a poor lady who went to visit a Buddhist temple, and wished to make a donation. However, she was so poor that she had only two cents, so she gave these to a monk. To her surprise, the temple's abbot himself came forth to help her repent for past offenses and dedicate her merits in front of the Buddha. Later on, the same lady was chosen to enter the imperial palace and became a concubine to the emperor. Clad in her riches, the lady once again went to the temple to donate, this time bringing thousands of silver pieces to give. To her dismay, the abbot only sent his disciple to help her dedicate her merits. The lady did not understand, and so questioned the abbot:

[Lady]: In the past, I only gave two cents in donation, and the Abbot personally helped me repent; today I come with great wealth to give, and the Abbot will not help

89

me perform my dedication, why is it so?

[Liao-Fan]: The abbot answered her saying:

[Abbot]: Though the money you gave in the past was scant, it came from a true and sincere heart, and it was necessary for me to repay your sincerity by personally performing your dedications. Today, although your donation is manifolds more, the heart of giving is not quite as true and sincere as before. Therefore, it is fitting and enough that my disciple perform your dedications for you.

[Liao-Fan]: This is the example of how thousands of silver pieces are only considered as half goodness, and two cents as full.

[Liao-Fan]: Another example is of Li Jung, an immortal of the Han Dynasty. He was teaching his student, Dong-bing Lyu, the art of transforming steel into gold. They would use this gold to help the poor. Dong-bing asked his teacher:

[Dong-bing]: Will the gold ever change back

to steel again?

[**Liao-Fan**]: Li Jung answered him saying:

[**Li Jung**]: After five hundred years, it will return to its original form.

[**Liao-Fan**]: Dong-bing then said:

[**Mr. Lyu**]: In this case, I don't want to learn this art, it will harm those who possess the gold five hundred years from now.

[**Liao-Fan**]: In actuality, Li Jung was only testing the goodness of his student's heart, and happy with the results, he said:

[**Li Jung**]: To become an immortal, one must complete three thousand virtuous deeds. What you have just said came from a truly kind heart; your three thousand deeds are fulfilled!

[**Liao-Fan**]: This was another example of half goodness and whole goodness.

[**Liao-Fan**]: When we perform a kind deed, it

is best if we can do it out of our innermost sincerity, not seeking rewards or noting in our minds how much we have done. If we practice thus, then all our good deeds will reach fulfillment and success. If, instead, we always think of the deeds we have performed, looking for a reward of some kind, then no matter how diligently we practice in an entire lifetime, the deeds still be considered as half goodness.

[Narrator]: For example, when we donate money to the poor, we can practice what is called 'pure donation'. In this type of giving, we do not linger on the thought of 'I', who is giving; or dwell on the importance of the object I am giving away; or think of who the receiver is. We are simply giving, and it is out of true sincerity and respect. When we give with 'pure donation', then one *dou* of rice can bring boundless fortune, and the merit from giving one cent can wipe away the sins from a thousand kalpas.

[Liao-Fan]: If we always keep in mind the good we have done, and expect rewards for our actions, then even a donation of two hundred thousand gold pieces would still not bear us the reward of a fully good fortune. This is another way of explaining half goodness and full goodness.

[Liao-Fan]: What is big goodness and small goodness? Once there was a high ranking official named Jung-da Wei, who was led into the spirit world to be judged for his good and bad deeds. The judge there ordered for his records of good and evil to be brought out. When the records arrived, Jung-da was astounded at the courtyard full of his bad records, and at the single scroll which contained his good deeds. The official then ordered for the two to be weighed on the scale. Surprisingly, the bad records which had filled the courtyard were lighter than the single scroll of good deeds, which was only as thin as a chopstick. Jung-da asked the judge:

[Jung-da]: I'm barely forty years old, how could I have committed so many wrongdoings?

[Liao-Fan]: The judge answered him, saying:

[Judge]: When you give rise to a single thought that is improper, it is considered a bad offense there and then, it does not have to be carried out through action to be counted as a wrong. For example, when you see a pretty lady and give rise to improper thoughts, that is considered an offense.

[Liao-Fan]: Jung-da then asked him what was recorded in the single scroll of good deeds which outweighed the evil deeds. The judge replied:

[Judge]: Once the Emperor planned to build a great stone bridge, and you proposed against the project due to the hardship and toil it would cause the tens and thousands of people needed for the work. This is a copy of your proposal to the Emperor.

[Liao-Fan]: Jung-da said:

[Jung-da]: I did make the proposal, but the Emperor dismissed it and began the project anyway. My proposal had no effect on the matter at all, how can it bear so much weight against my numerous offenses?

[Liao-Fan]: The judge replied:

[Judge]: Although the Emperor did not take your suggestion, that one thought of kindness you bore for the tens and thousands of people was very great. If the Emperor had listened to you, then the good performed would be even greater.

[Liao-Fan]: Therefore, when one is determined to do good for the benefit of all people, then a small deed can reap great merits.

[Narrator]: If one thinks only about benefiting oneself, then even if many deeds of kindness are performed, the merit would still be small.

[Liao-Fan]: What is difficult goodness and easy goodness? The knowledgeable scholars of the past used to say:

[Scholar]: When one wishes to conquer one's greed and desires, one should start with the most difficult to overcome.

[Liao-Fan]: Fan-chr, a student of Confucius,

95

once asked his teacher how to cultivate one's humanity to its fullest. Confucius replied:

[Confucius]: "Start with what's most difficult to practice".

[Liao-Fan]: What Confucius meant by the most difficult, was to sever the selfish mind, and one should practice that by conquering what is most difficult for oneself to conquer. We should practice like the old teacher, Mr. Su of Chiangshi, who gave two years worth of salary to a poor family who owed money to the government. Thus he saved them from being torn apart should the husband be taken to prison.

[Narrator]: Another example is Mr. Jang from Her-bei; Mr. Jang saw an extremely poor man who had to mortgage his wife and child, and had no money for their redemption. If he was unable to pay for their return, the mother and child could both lose their lives.

[Liao-Fan]: Therefore, Mr. Jang gave his ten years of savings to the poor man so the family could be reunited.

[Narrator]: Such examples as Mr. Su and Mr. Jang are rare, for they have given what is most difficult to give, and what others could not sacrifice, they did so willingly.

[Liao-Fan]: Another example is Mr. Jin from Chiangsu Province. He was old and without any sons, so his neighbor offered their young daughter in marriage to him, to give him descendants to carry on his lineage. But Mr. Jin could not bear to ruin the otherwise bright and long future of this young girl, and so refused the offer and sent her back home.

[Narrator]: This is another example of being able to overcome what is most difficult to conquer in oneself Therefore, the heavens showered down fortune which was especially good for these three old men.

[Liao-Fan]: It is easier to accumulate merit and virtue for those who have money and power than for those who are poor. But if one refuses to cultivate kindness even when it's easy and when one has the chance

to do so, then it would truly be a shame.
For those who are poor and without prestige,
doing kind things for others is a great
difficulty; but if in this difficulty one
can still manage to help others, then it is
a great virtue, and the merits gained would
be boundless.

[Liao-Fan]: In being a moral person and
dealing with affairs, we should help others
whenever the opportunity presents itself.
You should know that helping others is not
such an easy task, and that there are many
ways to do it. In short, the ways of helping
others can be simplified into ten important
categories. The first is 'supporting the
practice of kindness';

[Narrator]: When we see people trying to do
a little kindness, we should assist them in
their deeds and help their kindness grow.
When we see others who wish to do good but
cannot accomplish it on their own, we
should lend a hand and help them succeed.
This is the way we can cultivate
'supporting the practice of kindness'.

[Liao-Fan]: The second category is

'harboring love and respect":

[Narrator]: We should harbor respect towards those who are more knowledgeable, older, or of higher status than we are. For those who are younger, less fortunate, or of lower status, we should harbor a mind of loving care.

[Liao-Fan]: The third category is 'helping others succeed':

[Narrator]: When we see a person who is considering whether or not to do a good deed, we should persuade him to put all his effort into doing it. When others meet with difficulties in practicing kindness, we should help think of ways to overcome the difficulty and guide them to success. We must not be jealous at the accomplishments of others, nor try to sabotage their good acts.

[Liao-Fan]: The fourth category is 'persuading others to practice kindness':

[Narrator]: When we meet a person who is doing evil, we should tell him that doing

99

evil will only result in great suffering and painful retribution, and that he should avoid doing so at all costs. We should tell people who refuse to practice kindness or are only willing to practice a little kindness, that doing kind deeds will definitely have its rewards, and that kindness not only has to be cultivated, but must be cultivated constantly and on a large scale.

[Liao-Fan]: The fifth category is 'helping those in desperate need' :

[Narrator]: Most people tend to give when there is no need to give and refuse to give when there really is a need. When we meet people who are in great difficulties, emergencies, or dangers, we should lend them a hand and help in whatever way we can to bring them out of their difficult times. The merits accrued from helping others in times of desperate need are boundless indeed. However, one should not become proud and conceited for doing such deeds.

[Liao-Fan]: The sixth category is 'developing public projects for the greater benefit of the people':

[Narrator]: Projects which will bring great benefit to the public usually have to be performed by those with great influence and power. If a person has this capacity, such as rebuilding the water system or assisting a disaster area, then he ought to do it for the benefit of the general public. Those without such influence and power can do great deeds, too. For example, when one sees a small leak in the dam, one can use pebbles and dirt to stop the water and prevent disastrous flooding. Though this act may be small, the effect will not go unnoticed.

[Liao-Fan]: The seventh category is 'giving through donation':

[Narrator]: People of this world love, seek, and even die for money. Who is actually willing to help others by giving their own money away? When we recognize the difficulty involved in donation, we can come to appreciate the rarity of the man who willing to give for the purpose of helping others in need. He is an even greater man in the eyes of the poor. According to the law of cause and effect, 'those who give will in turn receive', and 'those who refuse to give will not receive'. When we cultivate one share of kindness, we will receive one share of fortune, there is no need to worry about having nothing left when we give to help others.

[Liao-Fan]: The eighth category is 'protecting the proper teachings':

[Narrator]: This is referring to the teachings of different religions. We must be able to differentiate between proper religions and deviant religions, and between proper teachings and deviant teachings. The teachings of deviant religions do great harm to people's minds and hearts, and naturally should be abolished. On the other hand, teachings with proper wisdom and views, such as that of Buddhism, which promotes kindness and goodness in society, should be supported. If one happens to see others in the act of destroying such proper teachings, one must put forth a complete effort to protect and uphold these teachings.

[Liao-Fan]: The ninth category is 'respecting our elders':

[Narrator]: Anyone who is deeply learned, knowledgeable, has high prestige, or is older than us is considered to be an elder, and should be highly regarded and respected.

[Liao-Fan]: The tenth category is 'loving and cherishing all living things':

[Narrator]: We should feel sympathy for all living creatures, even the tiny ants, who know of suffering and are afraid to die. How can we kill and eat living beings and not feel the least sorry? Some people even say that these things were meant for human consumption, but there is no logic in this argument, and it is only an excuse for those who desire meat.

[Liao-Fan]: I have only explained the above ten categories in summary, now I will explain each in detail and example:

[Liao-Fan]: What is meant by "supporting

the practice of kindness"? In the Yu Dynasty, there once was an emperor by the name of Shwun. One day, before he became emperor, Shwun was watching some fishermen on Lake Lei-ze. He noticed that all the younger and stronger fishermen took the spots where the water was deep and the fish were abundant, while the older and weaker fishermen were left with the rapids and shallow water, where there were very few fish. When Shwun saw this situation, he felt sympathy for the older and weaker fishermen, and thought of a way turn the situation around. He decided to join in the fishing party to set an example for the others. Whenever he saw fishermen plunder good fishing spots, he would conceal their faults and never even spoke of that their selfishness. When he saw those who were humble and yielding, he praised them everywhere he went and even followed their humble and polite ways. Shwun stayed and fished like this for a whole year until the other fishermen got into the habit of yielding good fishing spots to others.

[Narrator]: This story of Shwun is only an example to show how a person influences others through his actions, and not through his speech. It is not meant to encourage people to fish, because fishing is an act of killing. Please refrain from sports which take the lives of others.

[Liao-Fan]: A wise and intelligent man such as Shwun could have easily influenced others with a few words of advice. Why didn't he just say something instead of personally joining the gathering? You should understand that Shwun didn't want to use words, but preferred to set an example for others through his own actions. Shwun wanted those fishermen to feel ashamed of their own selfish behavior and change on their own accord. This really shows how deep and sincere Shwun's wish was for others to practice kindness.

[Liao-Fan]: In today's era of low morality, social breakdown, and loss of proper thinking, it is most difficult to find a good standard of behavior. Therefore, when those around us have shortcomings,

[Narrator]: We should not use our good points to highlight their deficiencies.

[Liao-Fan]: When the other person is unkind,

[Narrator]: We should not use our kindness to measure or compare ourselves to them.

[Liao-Fan]: When others are not as capable as we are,

[Narrator]: We should not purposely surpass them with our abilities.

[Liao-Fan]: Even when we are intelligent and competent, these skills should be kept hidden and not boasted of. Instead, we should behave even more humbly than ever. We should look upon our skills and abilities as unimportant, false, and unreal. When someone makes a mistake, we should tolerate it and conceal it, giving them a chance to reform without losing their self-respect. When we let the person keep his dignity, he will be even more careful of his actions in the future. When we see strengths and kindness in others, we should learn from them, praise them, and make their goodness known to others. In daily life, we should refrain from speaking and acting with selfish intentions, but instead seek to benefit society and the public. We can make beneficial laws and regulations for the public to follow.

[Narrator]: These are the qualities of a great man, since he thinks of the public welfare as more important than his own.

[Liao-Fan]: What is meant by "harboring love and respect for others"? Sometimes it is hard to tell from appearance whether a person is a gentleman or a scoundrel, since scoundrels can pretend to be gentlemen. The difference lies in their intentions: A gentleman's intentions are good, and a scoundrel's intentions are wicked. There is a great distance between the two, and they are as different as black and white. Mencius has said,

[Mencius]: The difference between gentlemen and common people lies in their intentions.

[Liao-Fan]: A gentleman's heart is only filled with love and respect for others.

There are thousands of different types of people in this world, some close to us, some strangers, some in high class and some in low, some smart while others are not, and some virtuous and some sinful, but nevertheless, they are our fellow mankind. They are like us, alive in flesh and blood, and they have feelings. There isn't a single person whom I should hate and disrespect. When your hearts are full of love and respect for others, it is the same as if your heart is full of love and respect for the saints and sages. When you understand others, it is the same as if you understand the saints and sages. Why?

[Narrator]: Because all the saints and sages want the people on this earth to lead happy, productive lives.

[Liao-Fan]: Therefore, if we can love and respect people and make them peaceful and happy, we are doing the job of a saint or sage.

[Liao-Fan]: What is meant by "helping others to succeed"? If we cast away raw jade, then this stone would be like any other worthless stone.

[Narrator]: But if we were to carve and polish it, it could be transformed into a priceless jewel.

[Liao-Fan]: It is the same with people. A person needs to be taught and guided, just as a jade needs to be carved and polished. When we see someone whom we feel has good potentials doing a good deed or working towards a proper goal, we should guide, support, praise, and encourage him, helping him succeed in his endeavors. If he is ever wrongly accused by another, you should try to clear his name and share his burden of slander. Only when you have helped him stand on his feet and be a part of good society would you have fulfilled your share of responsibility in helping others to succeed.

[Liao-Fan]: Most people dislike those who are different from them, such as a scoundrel versus a gentleman, and a bad person versus a good person. In villages; there are usually more bad people than virtuous ones.

[Narrator]: Since there are always more bad people around, a good person is often being taken advantage of; therefore a good person often has a hard time standing on his own.

[Liao-Fan]: Frankness and modesty are the usual characteristics of good people, they do not care much for their appearance. On the other hand, an average uneducated person often only pays attention to another's outer appearance. They like to gossip and make accusations; so, striving to do good turns out to be quite a challenge. A good person can easily be wrongly accused. When this happens, it is entirely up to the goodness and virtue of an elder to correct the actions of those who are bad and guide them back to the right track.

[Narrator]: It is also up to these elders to protect and help those who are good and need to stand on their own. The highest merit is achieved by those who can preserve good and rid evil.

[Liao-Fan]: What is meant by "persuading others to practice kindness"? As humans, we all have a conscience, but chasing after wealth and fame has kept us constantly busy and forgetful of our good conscience. We have become willing to stoop very low as long there is something to be gained from it. When a friend is about to ignore his good conscience to do something unworthy, we must remind and warm him, hoping to wake him from his muddled state of mind.

[Narrator]: It is like waking up someone when they're having a nightmare, it is up to us shake them into reality. When a person is undergoing a long spell of depression, we have to pull him out of it and help him clear his mind.

[Liao-Fan]: You are most virtuous if you can treat your friends with such kindness. A scholar named Han once said:

[Scholar Han]: By word of mouth, one can only persuade and influence another momentarily. It is easily forgotten with the passing of time and events. No one else would have heard what you have said. If you can persuade and influence others through written works, your words can be passed on for hundreds of generations around the world. Therefore, writing to promote virtue is an act of great speech, and is a most virtuous deed.

[Liao-Fan]: Here we talked about how we can persuade others by word of mouth and by writing books to promote virtue. Compared with the previous category of helping others to succeed, this is much more direct and obvious. However, the treatment of an illness with the right medicine sometimes proves to have special effects; therefore, we should not give up.

[Narrator]: It is also important how we do it. For instance, if a person is too stubborn, you should not persuade him with words. If you do, then you are wasting both your words and energy. If a person is gentle and willing to listen, but you fail to persuade him, then you have just missed a golden opportunity to do good. Either way is because you are not wise enough to tell the difference. You should then reflect to see what you did wrong so next time you will do it right and won't waste any more words or lose another opportunity.

[Liao-Fan]: What is meant by "helping those in desperate need"? During one's lifetime, a person often will suffer from serious problems, financial troubles, or separation from loved ones. If we meet someone like that, we should help that person as if we are the one who is experiencing the suffering. We should immediately come to his aid. If a person has been wrongly accused or convicted, we should plead for this person's innocence as well as aid him in any way we can. Scholar Suai once said,

[Scholar Suai]: It does not matter whether a favor is big or small; what counts is that it's done at a time when others need it most.

[Liao-Fan]: What humane words!

[Liao-Fan]: What is meant by "developing public projects for the greater benefit of the people"? Small construction works are needed for villages and big construction jobs are needed for cities. Public projects are anything that needs to be constructed for the public welfare,

[Narrator]: Such as: irrigation systems for farm lands, dams, bridges, or giving food and water to those who are hungry or thirsty.

[Liao-Fan]: Whenever you have the opportunity, you need to persuade others to put out their share of effort as well. Even when others slander or talk behind your back, you should not be deterred. Don't be afraid of what others might say about you, and don't get scared when the job gets tough. You should not let people's jealousy and hatred shake your resolve to do kind deeds.

[Liao-Fan]: What is meant by "giving through donation"? In Buddhism, giving is considered foremost in all practices of kindness. When one truly understands the meaning of giving and is willing to give away all his worldly belongings, even to the point of donating parts from his own body, then he is walking the way of the Buddha. A person who understands this principle would be willing to give away anything, even to the point of donating his eyes, ears, nose, tongue, body, and mind.

[Narrator]: For instance, in a past life, Shakyamuni Buddha offered his own body as food for a hungry tiger.

[Liao-Fan]: One can also give away the sight, sound, smell, taste, touch, and dharma. There is nothing a person cannot give away if he or she's willing.

[Narrator]: If a person can do this, then he is on his way to gaining purity of mind and body. He will have no worries or afflictions; Just like the Buddha.

[Liao-Fan]: When we find ourselves unable to give away everything, we can start by donating money. Worldly people treat their clothing and food as dearly as their lives. Therefore, monetary donation is most important for them.

[Narrator]: When we practice giving without hesitation, we can cure miserliness and at the same time help others in need.

[Liao-Fan]: However, it is not an easy thing to do. It's a difficult task at first, but will become natural the more we give. From cultivating giving, peace of mind can be attained, and then there is nothing you cannot give away.

(Narrator): This is the best way to cure a bad case of selfishness and an opportunity to change our attitudes toward money and worldly possessions.

(Liao-Fan): What is meant by "protecting the proper teachings"?

(Narrator): For millions of years, the proper teachings of religion has been a standard of truth and a spiritual guide for all living beings.

(Liao-Fan): If we don't have good doctrines, how can we join in and support the interplay of heaven and earth? How can people of all walks of life succeed in their endeavors without a standard to live by? How would we be able to escape from delusion and life's bondages? How would we create and arrange worldly affairs and transcend the cycle of birth and death?

[Narrator]: These all depend on good and proper teachings as the lighted path.

[Liao-Fan]: Therefore, whenever you see temples, memorials of past saints or sages, pictures of sages, or Buddhist texts, you should be respectful. If they are in need of repair, you should repair and put them back in order. We should especially tell people about the teachings of Buddha and widely spread the proper teachings. We should let others know of its value, in this way we are also showing our gratitude towards the Buddhas and sages. We need to do all we can to make this goal come true.

[Liao-Fan]: What is meant by "respecting our elders"? We should make an extra effort in showing our attention and respect towards parents, elder siblings, the governor, our superiors, or any elders of high virtue, prestige, and learning.

[Narrator]: When taking care of parents at home, we should do it with love in our hearts and a gentle, accommodating appearance. We should not raise our voice but maintain a peaceful bearing. As we cultivate these virtues, they will become a part of us, and we will change into a mild-mannered person. This is the way we can touch the hearts of heaven and evoke a response.

[Liao-Fan]: When carrying out deeds for our superiors or the government, we should follow the rules even when we aren't obliged to. We shouldn't try to slack off just because our superiors don't know what we are doing. Before we convict someone of a crime, regardless of whether the crime is serious or not, we should investigate carefully and handle the case with justice; We should not abuse the power and rights given to us by our superiors.

[Narrator]: When you face the emperor, you should respect him with the same respect as if you were facing the heavens. This is the correct behavior handed down from our ancestors. It has a direct and important effect on your hidden goodness.

[Liao-Fan]: Look at all the families who practiced loyalty and filial piety. Their descendants prosper for a long time and have bright futures. Therefore, we should follow their example and practice with caution.

[Liao-Fan]: What is meant by "loving and cherishing all living things"? We should know that a heart of compassion is what makes a man. Mencius once said:

[Mencius]: A man is not human if he does not feel compassion.

[Liao-Fan]: A person in search of the virtue of mercy and kindness looks out for his heart of compassion. A person who wants to accumulate merits also cultivates a compassionate heart. A person with compassion is a kind, virtuous, and merciful person, while one without compassion for others is unkind and without morals. It stated in The Ethical Code of the Chu Dynasty:

[Narrator]: In January, when most animals are bearing young, female species are not to be used for sacrificial purposes.
[Liao-Fan]: Mencius once said:

(**Mencius**): A gentleman will not live near the kitchen.

(**Liao-Fan**): This is to protect a compassionate heart, since a lot of slaughtering is done in the kitchen. Therefore, our forefathers did not eat meat under four circumstances: First is if they heard the killing, second is if they saw the killing, third is if the animal was raised by them, and fourth is if the animal was killed for their sake. If you are not vegetarian but wish to cultivate compassion, then you can learn from our ancestors by eating less meat.

(**Narrator**): According to the Buddha's teachings, living beings are born as animals as a result of having accumulated bad karma in their previous lives. After they pay their dues in retribution, they can be born as humans again. If they are willing to cultivate as a man, they can even become Buddhas. The meat I eat today may be the flesh of a future Buddha. The animal we see today may have been a man in previous lives. It is then possible that this animal was my parent, wife, son, relatives or friends.

Presently, I am human and they are animals. To kill and eat them would be making enemies of those I used to love. If I eat them today, perhaps in the future they will become human again while I become an animal due to my sins of killing. In their revenge, I will have to undergo the same suffering of being killed and eaten. When we think thus, how dare we kill? How can we swallow a morsel of that flesh? Besides, even if the meat does taste good, the taste only lasts from the mouth to the throat. After we swallow, there is nothing left to taste. There is no difference between eating meat and vegetables, why would you want to kill when there's no good behind it?

(Liao-Fan): Even if you cannot quit eating meat altogether, you should still try to gradually reduce your meat intake until vegetarianism is accomplished. In this way, you can reach a higher state of compassion within your heart. We should refrain from killing any living creature, even insects. Man makes silk from the cocoons of silkworms. The cocoons have to be boiled in water first, with the silkworms inside.

Think about it, how many silkworms lose

their lives in the process? When we cultivate the land for farming, how many insects have to be killed? Are you aware of the cost of lives involved in our everyday food and clothing? We kill to support ourselves. Therefore, we should be conservative and cherish the food and clothing we have. To waste them would create the same sin as killing. How often have we unknowingly harmed or stepped on a living creature? With a little awareness, we can prevent this from happening. Tung-pwo Su, a great poet from the Sung Dynasty once wrote:

[Narrator]: ' In love of the mice, we often leave him some rice; In pitying the moth, we won't light the lamp.'

[Liao-Fan]: What a kind and compassionate statement!

[Liao-Fan]: There are infinite types of goodness, I cannot mention them all. As long as you can expand on the ten previous categories, you can make them into a multitude of good deeds and virtues.

📖 The Fourth Lesson:
   The Benefit of the Virtue of Humility

[Narrator]: *The third lesson taught us the ways to accumulate kind deeds. Naturally, it would be best if people would practice kindness, but as humans, we are social beings. It is impossible to not come in contact with others in society; therefore, it is important to know the ways to improve our persons in dealing with others. The best way to do this is to follow the virtue of humility. A humble person in society receives support and trust from the general public. If a person understands the virtue of humility, he is the person who also understands the importance of constant self improvement. This constant self improvement not only includes the search for higher knowledge, but also encompasses the need to be more humane, better performance in daily duties, and improved communication with friends. Many benefits and rewards result from behaving with an understanding of humility. This lesson focuses on the benefits of virtue and humility, proven by Liao Fan's own experiences. You will be greatly benefited if you can thoroughly contemplate and understand these teachings.*

[Liao-Fan]: In the I Ching/Book of Change, the hexagram of Humility stated,

[Narrator]: The law of heaven takes from those who are arrogant and benefits those who are humble. The law of earth will not allow those who are conceited or self-content to always remain that way, but will bring change upon them. The humble will not wither, but shall be replenished, just as flowing water fills up lower places on the ground as it passes by, making up the differences. The law of spirits and gods bring harm to those who are arrogant and fortune to those who are humble. Even the laws of men despise the arrogant and like the humble.

[Liao-Fan]: Therefore, heaven, earth, spirits, gods, and people all prefer humility over arrogance. In the I Ching/Book of Change, the sixty four hexagrams talk about the constant changes and interactions of heaven and earth, ying and yang. The book teaches a person how to become more humane. Every hexagram contains both good and bad outcomes. The bad outcomes of a hexagram warn people to stop doing evil and to practice kind deeds. The good outcomes of a hexagram encourages people to diligently improve themselves and strive to be better. Only the Humility hexagram contains all good outcomes and no bad outcomes. The Chinese <u>Book of History</u> has also said,

[**Narrator**]: A person's arrogance will bring him harm; and his humbleness will bring him benefit.

[**Liao-Fan**]: I often went to take the exams accompanied by others, and every time I would meet scholars who were very poor. I noticed that before they succeeded in passing the exams and became prosperous, their faces showed such humility, peace, and harmony that I felt I could almost hold that quality in my hands.

[**Liao-Fan**]: Several years ago, I took my imperial exam in Beijing. Among the ten applicants from my village, Ching-Yu Ding was the youngest and extremely humble. I told one of the applicants, Jin-Po Fay; that this young man would definitely pass the exam this year. Jin-Po Fay asked,

[**Jin-Po**]: How can you tell?

[**Liao-Fan**]: I said, 'Only those who are humble are qualified to receive fortune. My friend, look at the ten of us; is there anyone as honest, generous, and never tries to come in first, as Ching-Yu? Do you see anyone who is always respectful, tolerant, careful and humble like Ching-Yu? Do you see anyone like Ching-Yu, who, when he is insulted, does not talk back, or who, when he is slandered, does not argue? Any person who can achieve such a level of humility will receive protection from the heaven, earth, and spirits. There is no reason he will not become prosperous.'

[**Narrator**]: Sure enough, when the test results came out, Ching-Yu Ding passed.

[**Liao-Fan**]: One year in Beijing, I was staying with my childhood friend, Kai-Zhi Fung. I noticed that he always carried himself in a humble way, and had a kind and

126

accommodating appearance. He was not a bit arrogant, which was an immense change from his childhood ways. Kai-Zhi had a friend named Ji-Yen Li who was straightforward and honest. Ji-Yen often scolded him on his mistakes, but Kai-Zhi always accepted the accusations calmly without talking back. I told him, "Just as there are signs which warn of coming misfortune, we can see that prosperity comes to those who have cultivated the cause for it. Heaven will help those whose hearts are humble. You, my friend, will definitely pass the imperial examination this year!"

[Narrator]: Later on, he indeed passed the exam.

[Liao-Fan]: There was a young man from San-tong Province named Yu-Fong Zhou who passed the first level of imperial examinations before he was even twenty. Unfortunately, try as he might, he could not pass the succeeding exams. When his father was moved to another post in the government, Yu-Fong went with him, and came to greatly admire a well-known scholar in that village named Min-Wu Chian. Yu-Fong brought his own

127

essays to see this man. He had no idea that Mr. Chian would pick up his calligraphy brush and blot out his entire essay. Not only was Yu-Fong not angry, he sincerely accepted all of Mr. Chian's corrections and immediately changed his paper accordingly.

[Narrator]: A young man who could be that humble and showed such willingness to improve himself was very rare indeed. The following year, Yu-Fong passed the imperial examination.

[Liao-Fan]: One year, I went to the Capital to pay my respects to the Emperor. I met a scholar named Jian-Suo Hsia who had all the qualities of a great man without a trace of arrogance. I felt the intense aura of his virtue and humility all about him. When I returned home, I told my friend, "When heaven wants a person to prosper, it will first bestow him with wisdom. Wisdom can make a person honest and well-disciplined. Heaven has already bestowed Jian-Suo with wisdom, or he couldn't be that gentle, kind and good. Surely, heaven will now make him prosperous."

[Narrator]: Sure enough, when the test results came out, Jian-Suo passed the exam.

[Liao-Fan]: There was a scholar named Wei-Yan Chang from Jiang-ying who was very learned and wrote good essays. He was also very well-known among many scholars. One year he took his exam at Nanking and stayed at a Taoist temple. When the test results were posted, he found that he had not passed the exam. He became furious and loudly accused the examiner of being blind for not recognizing his obvious talents. At that time, a Taoist monk stood by smiling, and Wei-Yan immediately directed his anger towards the monk. The monk said to him,

[Monk]: Your essay must not be good!

[Liao-Fan]: Wei-Yan got even angrier and said,

[Wei-Yan]: How do you know it's not good when you haven't even read it?

[Liao-Fan]: The monk said,

[Monk]: I often hear people say that the

most important element in writing good essays is a peaceful heart and harmonious temperament. Your loud and angry accusations just of now clearly shows that your mind is certainly not at peace and your temperament is violent. How could you possibly write good essays?

[Liao-Fan]: Wei-Yan obliviously submitted to the Taoist's words and in turn asked him for his advice. The Taoist said,

[Monk]: Whether you pass or not depends on your fate. If you are destined not to pass, then no matter how good your paper is, you will still fail the exam. You yourself will have to make a few changes!

[Liao-Fan]: Wei-Yan asked,

[Wei-Yan]: How can I change it if it is predestined?

[Liao-Fan]: The monk replied,

[Monk]: Though the power to form your destiny lies in the Heavens, the right to recreate it is in yourself As long as you are willing to do kind deeds and cultivate hidden virtues, there is nothing you ask that you will not receive.

[Liao-Fan]: Wei-Yan said,

[Wei-Yan]: I am only a poor scholar. What good deeds can I possibly do?

[Liao-Fan]: The monk said,

[Monk]: Practicing kind deeds and accumulating hidden virtues all stem from the heart. As long as you constantly harbor the intent to practice kindness and accumulate virtues, your merits are infinite and boundless! Take the virtue of humility for example, it does not cost anything; why can't you be humble and reflect on your own essay instead of blaming the examiner for being unfair?

[Liao-Fan]: Wei-Yan Chang listened to the Taoist monk, and from then on, suppressed his arrogant ways. He became very mindful of his own actions and tried not to make mistakes. Everyday he put forth additional effort to do more good deeds and accumulate more merits. Three years later, he dreamed one night that he entered a very tall house, and saw a booklet that contained all the names of the applicants who passed the exam that year. He saw many blank lines. Unable to understand what it meant, he asked the person next to him,

(Wei-Yan): What is this?

(Liao-Fan): The person replied,

(Person): This is the booklet that contains all the names of the applicants who passed the exam this year.

(Liao-Fan): Wei-Yan asked,

(Wei-Yan): Why does it have so many blank lines?

(Liao-Fan): The person answered,

(Person): The spirits of the underworld check on the applicants every three years. Only the names of those who practice kind deeds and do not make mistakes are allowed to appear in this booklet. The blank lines used to bear the names of those who were supposed to pass the exam, but due to their recent offenses, their names have been erased.

[Liao-Fan]: Then, pointing to a line, the person said:

[Person]: Ah-ha, for the past three years you have been very careful and have exerted such self-control that you haven't made any mistakes. Perhaps you should fill this blank. I hope you will cherish this opportunity and take care not to make any mistakes!

[Narrator]: Sure enough, Wei-Yan passed the exam that year and placed 105th.

[Liao-Fan]: From the examples given above, we know that spirits and gods are always watching our behaviors from above.

[Narrator]: Therefore, we must immediately do whatever is beneficial to others and avoid doing whatever is violent, dangerous, and harmful to others.

[Liao-Fan]: These are all things I can decide for myself. As long as I harbor good intentions; refrain from evil-doings; don't offend the heaven, earth, spirits, and gods; humble myself, be tolerant and not arrogant; then the heaven, earth, spirits and gods will constantly have pity on me; only then will I have a foundation for my future prosperity. Those who are full of conceit are definitely not destined to be great men. Even if they do prosper, they will not be able to enjoy their fortune for long. Intelligent people would definitely not make themselves small and narrow-minded and refuse the fortune they are entitled to.

[Narrator]: Besides, those who are humble always increase their opportunities to learn. If a person is not humble, who would want to teach him?

[Liao-Fan]: Also, humble people are always willing to learn the strengths of others. When others perform good deeds, the humble person will learn and follow their examples. In this way, the kind deeds humble people accomplish are boundless! For those who wish to cultivate and improve upon their virtues, they especially, cannot do without the virtue of humility.

[Liao-Fan]: The ancients had an old saying,

[Narrator]: Those who have their hearts set on attaining success and fame, will surely attain success and fame. Those who have their hearts set on attaining wealth and position, will surely attain wealth and position.

[Liao-Fan]: A person who has great and far reaching goals is like a tree having roots. A tree with roots will eventually sprout into branches, flowers and, leaves. A person who has set down great and far reaching goals must humble himself in every thought and try to relieve another's burden even if the occurrence is as insignificant as a speck of dust.

[Narrator]: If you can reach this level of humility, you will naturally touch the hearts of heaven and earth.

[Liao-Fan]: Furthermore, I am the creator of my own prosperity; if I truly want to

135

create it, I will certainly succeed. Look at the applicants who sought for fame and wealth, in the beginning, they did not harbor a sincere heart; it was only a passing notion. When they fancied it, they sought it. When their interest dropped, they stopped. Mencius once told Emperor Shuan Chi,

[Mencius]: Your Highness has a love for music. But your love for music is only a personal pleasure. If you can expand from the heart which seeks after personal happiness to that of sharing happiness with all your subjects, and make them just as happy as you are, then, surely the nation is bound to prosper!

[Liao-Fan]: I think it is the same for those who are seeking to pass the imperial exams. If a person can expand upon the heart which seeks to pass the exams to that of diligently doing kind deeds and accumulating merits, putting forth his best efforts to improve his character, then both destiny and prosperity are his to create.

Dear Listeners and Friends,

We hope you have benefited from listening to
Liao-Fan's Four Lessons and will acquire the same
spirit in creating your own destiny. We encourage
everyone to do their best in 'refraining from evil
and practicing kindness'. The teachings in Liao-Fan's
Four Lessons can lift the morale of the public and
transform our society into one of peace and harmony.
We welcome all interested parties to sponsor the
distribution of this audio book as teaching material
for schools and colleges. Let us all be a part in the
rebuilding of our children's morals and virtues. We
hereby announce that we do not reserve our copyrights,
and welcome all to reproduce and distribute this
audio book for the benefit of the general public.
Here at The *Foundation of Liao-Fan's Four Lessons*,
our goal is to promote the study and practice of these
teachings worldwide. Therefore, we will have
editions of this book in English, Chinese, etc.
Through understanding and practicing these teachings,
world peace is possible. We welcome your comments,
support, and sponsorship. Thank you very much!

Liao-Fan's Four Lessons Audio Book

Original work by Mr. Liao-Fan Yuan of the Ming Dynasty
Interpreted by Mr. Zhi-Hai Huang
Re-edited by Liao-Fan's Work Team
Sponsored and recorded by The Foundation of Liao-Fan's Four Lessons

Postscript

by Liao-Fan's Work Team

Congratulations on finishing Liao-Fan's Four Lessons. Hopefully it has awakened feelings of joy and virtue in your heart. The primary teaching of Liao-Fan is the accumulating of merit. There is a saying in China, "A person with virtue will keep his accumulated merit while a person without virtue will lose it." The survival and prosperity of the individual, the community and the nation is closely related to the merits generated by all members of the society. It is also said in China, "Those who do not understand the principles of Nature, or the law of cause and effect, will not grow in virtue." The ten principal virtues are: (generosity, morality, renunciation, wisdom, effort, patience, truthfulness, determination., loving-kindness, and equanimity.)

In modern society there are several problems. Hence we must begin a process of purification of the hearts and minds of the individual members of society. We emphatically believe that the teachings of Liao-Fan can stabilize the social order and purify the people's mind. It is our great hope that the social elites and the public functionaries will promote the Liao-Fan's Four Lessons throughout the world. These tapes and books have been translated, published, and distributed by the Foundation of Liao-Fan's Four Lessons. The Foundation's goal is the widest possible spreading of Liao-Fan's teaching, and hence, there are no copyright restrictions. We welcome all interested parties to reprint and disseminate Liao-Fan's Four Lessons free of charge. We believe this will have a broad and deep influence on the growth of world peace. The funding of these books and tapes comes from private donations. The donation for the awakening of mankind is the highest donation. These donations have been given in the spirit of Han Yu, the noted scholar of Tiang Dynasty, who said: "To awaken people once, one uses the mouth; while to awaken mankind for one hundred generations, one writes books." For those who want to further study the teachings of Liao-Fan, we highly recommend listening to Ven. Jing K'ung's exposition (in Chinese) in 18 audio cassette tapes which are also produced by the Foundation. Thank you for reading this postscript and once again I would like to congratulate on your finishing the book. May all beings be peaceful and free from suffering.

了凡四訓有聲書英文版發行通告

　　「了凡四訓」這本書，係袁黃坤儀先生寫於西元一六〇三年教誡他兒子的「訓子文」。淨宗當代第十三祖印光大師極力提倡，他的弘化社，印送這本書約在百萬冊以上，由此可知，印祖對這部書的重視。而且還不斷提倡我們研究、實行、講說。本會承導師上淨下空老法師訓示，全力弘揚此書，期使人人深信因果，並可挽救劫難。因為，惟有斷惡修善、深信因果，才能化解、消除當前災難。

　　本會為了弘揚此書於全球，三年來已有華語版、台、客、廣東、童音等版本之廣播劇發行流通，近日特別委託馬來西亞淨宗學會，聘請專業人才，製作英文廣播劇，首版發行之後，咸認為效果頗佳，具有國際水準，將為英語系國家及學習英文人士所歡迎。

　　並使僑居在外的華人子弟，對中華文化已漸陌生的下一代，能輕鬆活潑的認識中華文化。如此，相信佛法一定能如雨後春筍般的弘揚徧布全球上每一角落、每一種族。使人人都能存好心、說好話、行好事、做好人。如是則「心淨國土淨，心平世界平」。

　　然本會能力有限，值此英文版有聲書流通

之初，懇祈十方大德共同發心，大量翻錄流通，使此「挽救劫運的第一法寶」遍及全球，共挽劫運，縱不能全挽，也能減輕延緩，於共業中成就不共的殊勝利益。

　　丞盼淨宗同仁，共同發心弘揚、實行！
　　順頌　　淨安

PS：貴學會翻錄時，請用本會出版的英文
　　 CD版，或與本會聯絡。而不宜使用
　　 錄音帶直接翻錄，會損音質。

1998年2月26日 了凡編輯小組 謹啓

了凡四訓白話篇　目錄

了凡四訓白話篇

明朝　袁了凡進士原著
民初　黃智海先生演述
了凡弘法學會整理

了凡四訓這本書，是中國明朝袁了凡先生所作的家訓，教戒他的兒子袁天啟，認識命運的真相，明辨善惡的標準，改過遷善的方法。以及行善積德謙虛種種的效驗；並且以他自己改造命運的經驗來「現身說法」；讀了可以使人心目豁開，信心勇氣倍增，並欲效法了凡先生，來改造自己的命運；實在是一本有益世道人心，轉移社會風氣不可多得的好書。

但是了凡四訓的原著，是用文言文寫的；對現代人而言，閱讀起來比較吃力，而且不太容易懂，民國初年的黃智海先

生，為了使這本書能讓大家受益，所以用白話文不厭其煩詳盡的註解，可以說是用心良苦，功德無量；黃先生的白話註解在民間流傳很廣，它的優點是內容豐富詳盡，缺點則或許是過於繁瑣些；而現代人比較缺乏耐心，可能會因此而影響讀這本書的興趣，以致在有形無形中，使這本好書的影響力減弱，實在很可惜！

所以王警官有見於此，於是發心加以整理，重新排版印刷，使得大家容易閱讀，心生歡喜；並由善心人士出資，根據王警官整理的「了凡四訓白話解釋精簡本」，錄製成『了凡四訓有聲書』；而了凡四訓白話篇，也就是有聲書的話稿。希望人人讀過之後，都能夠學習「了凡先生」改造命運的精神，來創造自己，以及社會國家，乃至全人類光明的前途。

第一篇　立命之學

所謂「立命」，就是我要創造命運，而不是讓命運來束縛我。本篇立命之學，就是討論立命的學問，講解立命的道理。

袁了凡先生將自己所經歷，所見到改造命運種種的考驗，告訴他的兒子；要袁天啓不被命運束縛住，並且應竭力行善，『勿以善小而不為』；也必須努力斷惡，『勿以惡小而為之』；如此，則一定可以改變自己的命運，所謂『斷惡修善』、『災消福來』，這是改造命運的原理。

【千人千般命呀！命命不相同，明朝袁了凡，本來命普通，遇到孔先生，命都被算中；短命絕後沒功名，前世業障真不輕，庸庸碌碌二十年，一生命數被算定，雲谷禪師來開示，了凡居士才轉命呀！才轉命。】

我童年的時候父親就去逝了，母親要我放棄學業，不要去考功名，改學醫，並且說：學醫可以賺錢養活生命，也可以救濟別人。並且醫術學得精，可以成為名醫，這是你父親從前的心願。

後來我在慈雲寺，碰到了一位老人，相貌非凡，一臉長鬚，看起來飄然若仙風道骨，我就很恭敬地向他行禮。這位老人向我說：你是官場中的人，明年就可以去參加考試，進學宮了，為何不讀書呢？

我就把母親叫我放棄讀書去學醫的緣故告訴他。並且請問老人的姓名，是那裏人，家住何處；老人回答我說：我姓孔，是雲南人，宋朝邵康節先生所精通的皇極數，我得到他的真傳。

照註定的數來講，我應該把這個皇極數傳給你。因此，我就領了這位老人到我家，並將情形告訴母親。母

了凡四訓白話篇

四

親要我好好的待他。並且說：這位先生既然精通命數的道理，就請他替你推算推算，試試看，究竟靈不靈。

結果孔先生所推算的，雖然是很小的事情，但是都非常的靈驗。我聽了孔先生的話，就動了讀書的念頭，和我的表哥沈稱商量。表哥說：我的好朋友郁海谷先生在沈友夫家裏開館，我送你去他那裏寄宿讀書，非常方便。於是我便收學生讀書。我送你去他那裏寄宿讀書，非常方便。於是我便拜了郁海谷先生為老師。孔先生有一次替我推算我命裏所註定的數；他說：在你沒有取得功名做童生時，縣考應該考第十四名，府考應該考第七十一名，提學考應該考第九名。

到了明年，果然三處的考試，所考的名次和孔先生所推算的一樣，完全相符。孔先生又替我推算終生的吉凶禍福。他說：那一年考取第幾名，那一年應當補廩生，那一年應當做貢生，等到貢生出貢後，在某一年，應當選為四川省的一個縣

長，在做縣長的任上三年半後，便該辭職回家鄉。到了五十三歲那年八月十四日的丑時，就應該壽終正寢，可惜你命中沒有兒子。

這些話我都一一的記錄起來，並且牢記在心中。從此以後，凡是碰到考試，所考名次先後，都不出孔先生預先所算定的名次。唯獨算我做廩生所應領的米，領到九十一石五斗的時候才能出貢。那裡知道我吃到七十一石米的時候，學臺屠宗師（學臺：相當於現在的教育廳長）他就批准我，補了貢生。我私下就懷疑孔先生所推算的，有些不靈了。

後來果然被另外一位代理的學臺楊宗師駁回，不准我補貢生。直到丁卯年，殷秋溟宗師看見我在考場中的「備選試卷」沒有考中，替我可惜，並且慨嘆道：這本卷子所做的五篇策，竟如同上給皇帝的奏摺一樣。像這樣有大學問的讀書人，怎麼

可以讓他埋沒到老呢？

於是他就吩咐縣官，替我上公事到他那裏，准我補了貢生，經過這番的波折，我又多吃了一段時間的廩米，算起來連前所吃的七十一石，恰好補足，總計是九十一石五斗。我因為受到了這番波折，就更相信：一個人的進退功名浮沉，都是命中註定。而走運的遲或早，也都有一定的時候，所以一切都看得淡，不去追求了。

等我當選了『貢生』，按照規定，要到北京的國家大學去讀書。所以我在京城裏住了一年。一天到晚，靜坐不動，不說話，也不轉動念頭。凡是文字，一概都不看。到了己巳年，回到南京的國家大學，在沒有進國家大學以前，先到棲霞山去拜見雲谷禪師，他是一位得道的高僧。

我同禪師面對面，坐在一間禪房裏，三天三夜，連眼睛都

沒有閒。雲谷禪師問我說：凡是一個人，所以不能夠成為聖人，祇因為妄念，在心中不斷地纏來纏去；而你靜坐三天，我不曾看見你起一個妄念，這是什麼緣故呢？

我說：我的命被孔先生算定了，何時生，何時死，何時得意，何時失意，都有個定數，沒有辦法改變。就是要胡思亂想得到什麼好處，也是白想；所以就老實不想，心裡也就沒有什麼妄念了。雲谷禪師笑道：我本來認為你是一個了不得的豪傑，那裏知道，你原來只是一個庸庸碌碌的凡夫俗子。

我聽了之後，便請問他此話怎講？雲谷禪師說道：一個平常人，不能說沒有胡思亂想的那顆意識心；既然有這一顆一刻不停的妄心在，那就要被陰陽氣數束縛了；既被陰陽氣數束縛，怎麼可說沒有數呢？雖說數一定有，但是只有平常人，纔會被數所束縛住。若是一個極善的人，數就拘他不住

了。

因爲極善的人，儘管他的命數裏註定吃苦；但是他做了極大的善事，這大善事的力量，就可以使他苦變成樂，貧賤短命，變成富貴長壽。

而極惡的人，數也拘他不住。因爲極惡的人，儘管他本來命中註定要享福，但是他如果做了極大的惡事，這大惡事的力量，就可以使福變成禍，富貴長壽變成爲貧賤短命。

你二十年來的命都被孔先生算定了，不曾把數轉動一分一毫，反而被數把你給拘住了。一個人會被數拘住，就是凡夫，這樣看來，你不是凡夫，是什麼呢？

我問雲谷禪師說：照你說來，究竟這個數，可以逃得過什麼？禪師說：命由我自己造，福由我自己求；我造惡就自然折福；我修善，就自然得福。從前各種詩書中所說，實在是的的

確確，明明白白的好教訓。我們佛經裏說：一個人要求富貴就得富貴，要求兒女就得兒女，要求長壽就得長壽。

只要做善事，命就拘他不住了。因為說謊是佛家的大戒，那有佛菩薩還會亂說假話，欺騙人的呢？

我聽了以後，心裏還是不明白，又進一步問說：孟子曾說：凡是求起來，就可以得到的，這是說在我心裏可以做得到的事情。

若是不在我心裏的事，那麼怎能一定求得到呢？譬如說道德仁義，那全是在我心裏的，我立志要做一個有道德仁義的人，自然我就成為一個有道德仁義的人，這是我可以盡力去求的。若是功名富貴，那是不在我心裏頭的，是在我身外的，要別人肯給我，我才可以得到。倘若旁人不肯給我，我就沒法子得到，那麼我要怎樣才可以求到呢？雲谷禪師說：孟子的話不

錯，但是你解釋錯了。你沒看見六祖慧能大師說：所有各種的福田，都決定在各人的心裏。福離不開心，心外沒有福田可尋，所以種福種禍，全在自己的內心。只要從心裏去求福，沒有感應不到的！

能向自己心裏去求，那就不只是心內的道德仁義，可以求得，就是身外的功名富貴，也可以求到，所以叫做內外雙得。換句話說，爲了種福田而求仁求義，求福，求祿，是必有所得的。

一個人命裏若有功名富貴，就是不求，也會得到；若是命裏沒有功名富貴，就算是用盡了方法，也求不到的。

所以一個人，若不能自己檢討反省，而只是盲目地向外面追求名利福壽；但得到得不到，還是聽天由命，自己毫無把握。這就合了孟子所說，求之有道，得之有命的兩句話了。

要知道縱然得到，究竟還是命裏本來就有的，並不是自己求的效驗，所以可以求到的，繞去求，求不到的，就不必去亂求。

倘若你一定要求，那不但身外的功名富貴求不到，而且因為過份的亂求，過份的貪得，為求而不擇手段，那就把心裏本來有的道德仁義，也都失掉了，那豈不是內外雙失麼？所以亂求是毫無益處的。

【求富貴呀得富貴，求兒女呀得兒女，求長壽呀得長壽，沒有什麼求不到呀，求不到！只要做好事，從心裏去求，心就是福田呀，千萬別亂求；心就福田呀，千萬別亂求。】

雲谷禪師接著再問我說：孔先生算你終身的命運如何？

我就把孔先生算我，某年考的怎麼樣，某年有官做，幾歲就要死的話詳詳細細的告訴他。雲谷禪師說：你自己想想，你

應該考得功名麼？應該有兒子麼？我反省過去所作所為，想了很久才說：我不應該考得功名，也不應該有兒子。因為有功名的人，大多有福相。

我的相薄，所以福也薄。又不能積功德積善行，成立厚福的根基。並且我不能忍耐，擔當瑣碎繁重的事情。別人有些不對的地方，也不能包容。因為我的性情急燥，肚量窄小。有時候我還自尊自大，把自己的才幹、智力，去蓋過別人。心裏想怎樣就怎麼做，隨便亂談亂講。像這樣種種舉動，都是薄福的相，怎麼能考得功名呢！

喜歡乾淨，本是好事；但是不可過分，過分就成怪脾氣了。所以說越是不清潔的地方，越會多生出東西來。相反地，很清潔的水反而養不住魚。

我過分地喜歡清潔，就變得不近人情，這是我沒有兒子的

第一種緣故。

天地間，要靠溫和的日光，和風細雨的滋潤，纔能生長萬物。我常常生氣發火，沒有一點和育之氣，怎麼會生兒子呢？這是我沒有兒子的第二種緣故。

仁愛，是生生的根本，若是心懷殘忍，沒有慈悲；就像果子一樣，沒有果仁，怎麼會長出果樹呢？所以說，忍是不會生養的根；我只知道愛惜自己的名節，不肯犧牲自己，去成全別人，積些功德，這是我沒有兒子的第三種緣故。

說話太多容易傷氣，我又多話，傷了氣，因此身體很不好，那裏會有兒子呢？這是我沒有兒子的第四種緣故。

人全靠精氣神三種才能活命；我愛喝酒，酒又容易消散精神；一個人精力不足，就算生了兒子，也是不長壽的，這是我沒有兒子的第五種緣故。

一個人白天不該不睡覺，晚上又不該不睡覺；我常喜歡整夜長坐，不肯睡，不曉得保養元氣精神，這是我沒有兒子的第六種緣故。其它還有許多的過失，說也說不完呢！雲谷禪師說：豈只是功名不應該得到，恐怕不應該得的事情，還多著哩！

當知有福沒福，都是由心造的。有智慧的人，曉得這都是自作自受；糊塗的人，就都推到命運頭上去了。

譬如這個世上能夠擁有千金產業的，一定是享有千金福報的人；能夠擁有一百金產業的，一定是享有一百金福報的人，一定是應該受餓死報應的人。比如說善人積德，上天就加多他應受的福。惡人造孽，上天就加多他應得的禍。上天不過就他本來的質地上，加重一些罷了，並沒有一絲毫別的意思。

接下來這段是雲谷禪師借俗人之見，來勸了凡先生努力積

德行善。

　就像生兒子，也是看下的種怎樣，種下的很厚，結下的果也厚。種下得薄，結的也薄。譬如一個人，積了一百代的功德，就一定有一百代的子孫，來保住他的福。積了十代的功德，就一定有十代的子孫，來保住他的福。積了三代或者兩代的功德，就一定有三代或者兩代的子孫，來保住他的福。至於那些只享了一代的福，到了下一代，就絕後的人；那是他功德極薄的緣故，恐怕他的罪孽，還積得不少哩！你既然知道自己的短處，那就應該把你一向不能得到功名，和沒有兒子的種種福薄之相，盡心盡力改得乾乾淨淨。一定要積德，一定要對人和氣慈悲，盡心盡力替人包含一切，而且要愛惜自己的精神。

　從前的一切一切，譬如昨日，已經死了；以後的一切一切切，譬如今日，剛剛出生；能夠做到這樣，就是你重新再生了

一個義理道德的生命了。我們這個血肉之軀，尚且還有一定的的數；而義理的、道德的生命，那有不能感動上天的道理？書經太甲篇上面說道：上天降給你的災害，或者可以避開；而自己若是做了孽，就要受到報應，不能愉快心安地活在世間上了。

詩經上也講：人應該時常想到自己的所作所為，合不合天道。很多福報，不用求，自然就會有了。因此，求禍求福，全在自己。

【書經說：天作孽呀，猶可違呀猶可違，自作孽呀，不可活呀，不可活；詩經上也說：常常想自己，所做跟所為，合不合天道，求禍與求福，全在你自己呀！全在你自己。】

孔先生算你，不得功名，命中無子，雖然說是上天註定，但是還是可以改變。你只要將本來就有的道德天性，擴充起

來，盡量多做一些善事，多積一些陰德，這是你自己所造的

福，別人要搶也搶不去，那有可能享受不到呢？

易經上也有為一些宅心仁厚、有道德的人打算，要往吉祥

的那一方去，要避開凶險的人，凶險的地方。

如果說命運是一定不能改變的，那末吉祥又何處可以趨，

凶險又那裡可以避免的呢？易經開頭第一章就說：經常行善的家

庭，必定會有多餘的福報，傳給子孫；這個道理，你眞的能夠

相信嗎？

我相信雲谷禪師的話，並且向他拜謝，接受他的指教；同

時把從前所做的錯事，所犯的罪惡，不論大小輕重，到佛前

去，全部說出來；並且做了一篇文字，先祈求能得到功名，還

發誓要做三千件的善事，來報答天地祖先生我的大恩大德。雲

谷禪師聽我立誓要做三千件的善事，就拿了功過格給我看。叫

了凡四訓白話篇

一八

我照著功過格所訂的方法去做，所做的事，不論是善是惡，每天都要記在功過格上，善的事情就記在功格下面，惡的事情就記在過格下面。

不過做了惡事，還要看惡事的大小，把已經記的功來減除。並且還教我唸準提咒，更加上了一重佛的力量，希望我所求的事，一定會有效應。雲谷禪師又對我說：有一種畫符籙的專家曾說：一個人如果不會畫符，是會被鬼神恥笑的。

畫符有一種秘密的方法傳下來，只是不動念頭罷了。當執筆畫符的時候，不但不可以有不正的念頭，就是正當的念頭，也要一齊放下。把心打掃得乾乾淨淨，沒有一絲雜念，因為有了一絲的念頭，心就不清淨了。到了念頭不動，用筆在紙上點一點，這一點就叫混沌開基，因為完整的一道符，都是從這一點開始畫起，所以這一點是符的根基所在。

從這一點開始一直到畫完整個符，若沒起一些別的念頭，那麼這道符，就很靈驗。不但畫符不可夾雜念頭，凡是禱告上天，或者是改變命運，都要從沒有妄念上去用工夫，這樣纔能感動上天。孟子講立命的道理說道：短命和長壽沒有分別。乍聽之下會覺得奇怪？因爲短命和長壽相反，而且完全不同，怎樣說是一樣呢？要曉得在一個妄念都完全沒有時，就如同嬰兒在胎胞裏面的時候，那曉得短命和長壽的分別呢？

等到出了娘胎，漸漸有了知識，有了分別的心；這時，前生所造的種種善業惡業，都要受報應了，那也就有短命和長壽的分別了。

因此；命運是自己造的。如果把立命這兩個字細分來講，那末富和貧要看得沒有兩樣，不可以富的仗著有錢有勢，隨便亂來，窮的也不可以自暴自棄去做壞事，儘管窮，仍然應該安

分守己的做好人；能夠這樣，纔可以把本來貧窮的命，改變成富貴的命。本來富貴的命，改變成更加富貴，或者是富貴得更長久。窮與通，要看得是沒有兩樣，不發達的人，不可因為自己不得志，就不顧一切，隨便荒唐；發達的人，也不可仗勢欺人，造種種的罪業，越是得意，越是要為善去惡，廣種福田。

能夠這樣，纔可以把本來窮苦的命，改變成發達的命，本來發達的命，就會更加發達了。短命和長壽，要看得沒有兩樣，不可說我短命；不久就死了，就趁還活著的時候，隨便做惡事，糟蹋自己。要曉得既然已生成短命，就更加應該做好人，希望來生不要再短命，這一生或許也可以把壽命延長一些哦！

命中長壽的人，不要認為自己有得活，就拼命造孽，做奸犯科，犯邪淫。要曉得長壽得來不易，更應該做好人，才可以

保住他的長壽呀。能夠明白這種道理，才可以把本來短的命變成長壽，本來長壽的命，更加長壽健康。人生在這個世界上，只有這生與死的關係最為重大，所以短命同了長壽，就是最重大的事情。既然說到這最重大的短命同了長壽，那末此外一切順境，富有和發達；逆境，貧窮和不發達，都可以包括在內了。

孟子講立命的學問，祇講到短命和長壽，並沒講到富和貧，發達和不發達，就是這個道理。

接著雲谷禪師又告訴我說：孟子所說的『修身以俟之』這句話，是說：自己要時時刻刻修養德行，不要做半點過失罪惡。至於命能不能改變，那是積德的事，求天的事。說到修字，那麼身上有一些些過失罪惡，就應該像治病一樣，把過失罪惡要完全去掉。講到俟，要等到修的功夫深了，

命自然就會變好，不可以有一絲一毫的非份之想，也不可以讓心裏的念頭亂起亂滅，都要完全把它斬掉斷絕，能夠做到這種地步，已經是達到先天不動念頭的境界了。到了這種功夫，那就是世間受用的眞正學問。

雲谷禪師接著又説：平常時一般人的行為，都是根據念頭轉的，凡是有心而為的事，不能算是自然，不著痕跡。你現在還不能做到不動心的境界，你若能念準提咒，不必用心去記或數遍數，只要一直念下去，不要間斷。念到極熟的時候，自然就會口裏在念，自己不覺得在念，這叫做持中不持；在不念的時候，心裏不覺的仍在念，這叫做不持中持；念咒能念到這樣，那就我、咒、念打成了一片，自然不會有雜念進來，那末念的咒，也就沒有不靈驗的了。但是這種功夫，一定要透過實踐，才能領會到的。

立命之學

二二三

我起初的號叫做學海，但是自從那一天起就改號叫做了凡；因為我明白立命的道理，不願意和凡夫一樣。把凡夫的見解，完全掃光，所以叫做了凡。

從此以後，就整天小心謹慎，自己也覺得和從前大不相同。從前儘是糊塗隨便，無拘無束；到了現在，自然有一種小心謹慎，戰戰兢兢戒慎恭敬的景象。

雖然是在暗室無人的地方，也常恐怕得罪天地鬼神。碰到討厭我，毀謗我的，我也能夠安然的接受，不與旁人計較爭論了。從我見了雲谷禪師的第二年，到禮部去考科舉。孔先生算我的命，應該考第三名，那知忽然考了第一名，孔先生的話開始不靈了。孔先生沒算我會考中舉人，那知道到了秋天鄉試，我竟然考中了舉人，這都不是我命裡註定的，雲谷禪師說：命運是可以改造的。這話我更加地相信了。

我雖然把過失改了許多，但是碰到應該做的事情，還是不能一心一意的去做，即使做了，依然覺得有些勉強，不太自然。自己檢點反省，覺得過失仍然很多。

例如看見善，雖然肯做；但是還不能夠大膽地向前拼命去做。或者是遇到救人時，心裡面常懷疑惑，沒有堅定的心去救人。自己雖然勉強做善事，但是常說犯過失的話。有時我在清醒的時候，還能把持住自己，但是酒醉後就放肆了。雖然常做善事，積些功德；但是過失也很多，拿功來抵過，恐怕還不夠，光陰常是虛度。從己巳年聽到雲谷禪師的教訓，發願要做三千件的善事；直到己卯年，經過了十多年，才把三千件的善事做完。

在那個時候，我剛和李漸庵先生，從關外回來關內，沒來得及把所做的三千件善事迴向。到了庚辰年，我從北京回到了

南方，方才請了性空、慧空、兩位有道的大和尚，借東塔禪堂完成了這個迴向的心願。到這時候，我又起了求生兒子的心願，也許下了三千件善事的大願。到了辛巳年，生了你，取名叫天啟。

我每做了一件善事，隨時都用筆記下來；你母親不會寫字，每做一件善事，都用鵝毛管，印一個紅圈在日曆上，或是送食物給窮人，或買活的東西放生，都要記圈。有時一天多到十幾個紅圈呢！也就是代表一天做了十幾件善事。

像這樣到了癸未年的八月，三千條善事的願，方纔做滿。又請了性空和尚等，在家裡做迴向。到那年的九月十三日，又起求中進士的願，並且許下了做一萬條善事的大願。到了丙戌年，居然中了進士，吏部就補了我寶坻縣縣長的缺。我做寶坻縣的縣長時，準備了一本有空格的小冊子，這本小冊子，我叫

它作治心篇。意思就是恐怕自己心起邪思歪念，因此，叫『治心』二字。

每天早晨起來，坐堂審案的時候，叫家裏人拿這本治心篇交給看門的人，放在辦公桌上。到了晚上，在庭院中擺了桌子，仿照宋朝的鐵面御史趙閱道，焚香禱告天帝，天天都是如此。你母親見我所做的善事不多，常常皺著眉頭向我說：我從前在家，幫你做善事，所以你所許下三千件善事的心願，能夠做完。現在你許了做一萬件善事的心願，在衙門裏沒什麼善事可做，那要等到什麼時候，才能做完呢？

在你母親說過這番話之後，晚上睡覺我偶然做了一個夢，看到一位天神。我就將一萬件善事不易做完的緣故，告訴了天神，天神說：『只是你當縣長減錢糧這件事，你的一萬件善

事，已經足夠抵充圓滿了。』

原來寶坻縣的田，每畝本來要收銀兩分三釐七毫，我覺得百姓錢出得太多，所以就把全縣的田清理一遍；每畝田應繳的錢糧，減到了一分四釐六毫，這件事情確實是有的；但也覺得奇怪，怎麼這事會被天神知道，並且還疑惑，只有這件事情，就可以抵得了一萬件善事呢？

那時候恰好幻余禪師從五台山來到寶坻，我就把夢告訴了禪師，並問禪師，這件事可以相信嗎？幻余禪師說：做善事要存心真誠懇切，不可虛情假意，企圖回報。那末就是只有一件善事，也可以抵得過一萬件善事了。況且你減輕全縣的錢糧，全縣的農民都得到你減稅的恩惠，千萬的人民因此減輕了重稅的痛苦，而獲福不少呢！

我聽了禪師的話，就立刻把我所得的俸銀薪水捐出來，請

二八

禪師在五台山替我齋僧一萬人，並且把齋僧的功德來迴向。

孔先生算我的命，到五十三歲時，應該有災難。我雖然沒祈天求壽，五十三歲那年，我竟然一點病痛都沒有。現在已經六十九歲了（多活了十六年）。書經上說：天道是不容易相信的，人的命，是沒一定的。又說：人的命沒有一定，是要靠自己創造的。

這些話，一點都不假。我由此方知，凡是講人的禍福，都是自己求來的，這些話實在是聖賢人的話；若是說禍福，都是天所註定的，那是世上庸俗的人所講的。

【天道不易信呀，人命沒一定，人命沒一定呀，要靠自己造；若說禍與福呀，都是天註定，那是凡夫與俗子，而非聖賢說的話呀，說的話！】

你的命，不知究竟怎樣？就算命中應該榮華發達，還是要

常常當作不得意想。就算碰到順當吉利的時候，還是要常常當

作不稱心，不如意來想。就算眼前有吃有穿，還是要當作沒錢

用，沒有房子住想。就算旁人喜歡你，敬重你，還是要常常小

心謹慎，做恐懼想。就算你家世代有大聲名，人人都看重，還

是要常常當做低微想。就算你學問高深，還是要常常當做粗淺

想。

這六種想法，是從反面來看問題，能夠這樣虛心，道德自

然會增進，福報也自然會增加。

講到遠，應該要想把祖先的德氣，傳揚開來；講到近，應

當想父母若有過失，要替他們遮蓋起來；這裏即是說明孟子的

『父為子隱，子為父隱』的大義所在；講到向上，應該要想報

答國家的恩惠；講到對下，應該要想造一家的福；說到對外，

應該要想救濟別人的急難；說到對內，應該要想預防自己的邪

念和邪想。

這六種想法，都是從正面來肯定問題，能夠常常如此的存心，必然能成為正人君子。

一個人必須要每天知道自己有過失，才能天天改過，若是一天不知道自己的過失，就一天安安逸逸的算自己沒過失。如果每天都無過可改，就是每天都沒有進步；天底下聰明俊秀的人實在不少，然而他們道德上不肯用功去修，事業不能用功去做；就只為了因循兩個字，得過且過，不想前進，所以才耽擱了他們的一生。

雲谷禪師所教立命的許多話，實在是最精，最深，最真，最正的道理，希望你要細細的研究，還要盡心盡力的去做，千萬不可把大好的光陰虛度過。

第二篇 改過之法

人，既然不是生下來就是聖人，那裏能沒有過失呢？孔子說：「過則勿憚改。」

只要有了過失，就不可以怕改。所以袁了凡先生在講過改造命運的道理方法後，就接著把改過的方法，詳細地說出來，教訓他的兒子袁天啓。這第二篇就是講改過的方法。小的過失，尚且要改；那末大的罪孽，自然就不會再造了。

在春秋時代，當時各國的高級官吏，常常要從一個人的言語、行爲、去加以判斷；就可以猜想到這個人可能遭遇到的吉凶禍福，並且沒有不靈驗的。這可以在左傳和國語這幾種書上看得到的。大凡吉祥和凶險的預兆，都在心裏發出根苗反應出來，雖然根苗是由心裏發出來的，但是會表現到全身的四肢

上，譬如一個人很厚道，那麼他的全身四肢都會顯得穩重。一個人刻薄，那麼他的全身四肢都會顯得輕佻。

一個人凡是偏在厚道的，一定時常近福；偏在刻薄的，一定時常近禍。一般人沒有見識，眼光像被一層膜給遮住了，甚麼都看不到；就說禍福沒有一定，而且是無法預測的。

一個人能夠做到極誠實，毫無半點虛假，這個人的心就可以與天心相合了，因此；能夠用誠心處人處事，福就會自然降臨。所以觀察一個人，只要看他的行為，都是善的，就可以預知他的福，就會來了。

相反的，觀察一個人，只要看他的行為，都是不善的，就可以預知他的禍，就要來了。人若是要得福，要遠離災禍；在沒有講到做善事前，先要把自己的過失改掉。

但改過的方法，第一要發『羞恥心』。想想古時候的聖

賢，和我一樣，都是男子漢、大丈夫，為什麼他們可以流芳百世，大家還要以他們做為師表榜樣；而我為什麼這一生就搞得身敗名裂呢？

這都是因為自己過份貪圖享樂，受到種種壞環境的污染，偷偷做出種種不應該做的事，自己還以為旁人不知道，目無國法，毫無慚愧之心；就這樣天天的沉淪下去，同禽獸一樣了，自己卻還不知道。

世界上，令人可羞可恥的事情，沒有比這個更大的了。孟子說：一個人最大的，最要緊的事情就是這個恥字。為什麼呢？因為曉得這個恥字，就會把自己的過失盡量改掉，就可以成為聖賢；若不曉得這個恥字，就會放肆亂來失掉人格，便和禽獸相同了。

這些話都是改過的真正秘訣。改過的第二個方法，是要發

了凡四訓白話篇

三四

戒慎恐懼的心。要知道天地鬼神，都在我們的頭上。

鬼神和我們不一樣，它們什麼都看得到，所以鬼神是不容易被欺騙的。我雖然在大家看不到的地方犯錯，但是天地鬼神，實際上就像鏡子那樣的照著我，把我的過失罪惡照得清清楚楚。過失就重的，就有種種的災禍，降到我的身上來；就算過失輕的，也要減損我現在的福報，我怎麼能夠不怕呢？

不只是像前面所說的而已。就是在自己家裡空閒的地方；但神明的監察，仍然是非常的厲害，非常的清楚。

我雖然把過失遮蓋得十分秘密，掩飾得十分巧妙；但是在神明看來，我的肺肝，早被看透，馬腳全露出來了。到最後還是沒有辦法欺騙自己，若是被旁人看破，這個人就一文不值了。又怎麼可以不時常存著一顆戒慎恐懼的心呢？

這還不只像上面所說的種種呢！一個人只要一口氣還在，

就算是犯下滔天的罪過，還是可以懺悔改過的。

古時候有個人，作了一輩子的惡事，到他快死的時候，忽然悔悟，發了一個很大的善念，就立刻得到好死。

這就是說，人若是在緊要關頭能夠轉一個非常痛切又勇猛的善念，便可以把百年所積的罪惡洗乾淨。譬如千年黑暗的山谷，只要有一盞燈照了進去；光到之處，就可以把千年來的黑暗，完全除去了。所以過失不論長久，或者是新犯的；只要能改，就是了不起。

雖然有過失只要改過就好，但是絕對不可以認為犯過可以改，就是常常犯也不要緊，這是萬萬不可以的。如果是這樣，就是有心犯過，罪就更加重了。

並且在這個不清淨的世間，是幻滅無常的，我們這個血肉之身，是非常容易死的；只要一口氣喘不過來，這個身體，就

不是我的了；到那個時候就是想要改，也沒法子改了。並且人死了後，什麼都帶不去；只有這個孽，是一定跟去的。

因此，明的報應，在陽間你要承擔千百年的惡名；雖然你有孝順的兒子，和可愛的孫子，也不能替你洗清惡名；暗的報應，在陰間，還要千百劫的時間，沉淪在地獄受無量無邊的大苦。雖然碰到聖人，賢人，佛菩薩也不能救助你，接引你，這樣怎麼能不怕呢？

第三，一定要發一直向前的勇猛心。一個人之所以有了過失還不肯改，都是因為得過且過，不能振作奮發，墮落退後的緣故。

要知道若是要改過，一定要起勁用力，當下就改，絕對不能夠拖延疑惑，也不可以今天等明天，明天等後天，一直拖下去。小的過失，像尖刺戳在肉裏，要趕緊挑掉拔掉。大的過

失，像毒蛇咬到手指頭一樣的厲害，要趕緊切掉手指頭，不可有絲毫的猶疑延遲的念頭；否則蛇毒在身中散開，人就會死。

就像易經中的益卦所講，風起雷動，萬物都生長起來，利益是這樣的大。這是比喻人若能夠改過遷善，其利益是最大的。

【改過要發心呀！改過要發心。發些什麼心呀！發些什麼心。第一要發那羞恥心，第二要發那敬畏心，第三要發那勇猛心，具備這三種心，便能有過立即改呀！立即改。】

一個人改過，如果能具備以上所說的羞恥心，敬畏心，勇猛心這三種心，那麼就能有過立刻改了，就像春天的薄冰，碰到太陽光一樣，還怕不融化嗎？但要改過，有三種方法。一種是從事實上改，一種是從道理上改，一種是從心念上改。

因為用這三種不同的功夫，所以得到的效驗，也自然不會

一樣。現在先從事實上改的這一句，來加以說明。

譬如前天殺了活的東西，今天起禁止不再殺了。前天發了火罵人，今天起禁止不再發火了。這種就是在事情的本身來改錯，禁止不再犯的方法。但是勉強壓住，不再犯，比自然而然的改，要難百倍。並且這犯過的病根沒有去掉，仍在心裏。雖然一時勉強壓住，終究還是要露出來的，就像東邊把它滅了，西邊又會冒出來一樣，這究竟不是徹底拔除乾淨的改過方法。

我再把從理上改過的方法加以說明；肯努力改過的人，在他沒有禁止做這件事之前，先要明白這事不能做的道理；譬如一個人，所犯的過失在殺生；那麼他先應該想到：上天有好生之德，凡是有生命的，都會愛惜生命而且怕死。殺它的生命，來養我的身體，自問心能安嗎？而且有些東西，雖已被殺，但是還沒有完全死，像魚和毛蟹之類。在半死半活的時候放進鍋

子裏燒，這樣的痛苦，一直要透到骨髓裏；你看罪過不罪過呢？而供養自己，就要用各種貴重的，味道好的東西，擺滿了一桌。雖然這樣地講究，但是一經吃過，便成渣滓，什麼都沒有了。要曉得人吃蔬菜素食素湯等等，也吃得飽啊！何必一定要去傷害生命，造殺生的罪孽，減少自己的福報呢？

又想，凡是有血氣有生命的東西，都有靈性知覺，既然都有靈性知覺，那麼和我都是一樣的了，就算是自己不能修到道德極高的地步，使他們都來尊重我，親近我，像古時候的聖人大舜，還在他種田的時候就有象替他犁田，鳥幫他拔草。又怎能天天傷害生命，使它們與我結仇，恨我到永無盡期呢？能想到這些，那就會面對桌上有血肉，有生命的菜餚，自然覺得傷心而不能下咽了。譬如像前天喜歡發怒，應該想到：人各有各的長處，也各有各的短處；碰到他人短處的地方，按照情理，

應該要哀憐他的苦惱，原諒他的短處；若是有人不講道理冒犯了我，那是錯在他，與我有什麼關係呢？本來就沒什麼怒可以發的呀！又想到：天下，絕對沒有自以為什麼錯都沒有的英雄豪傑，因為一個人自以為了不起，那是最笨的人。天下也絕對沒有怨恨旁人的學問；因為人若是真正有學問，就會更加謙虛；而且能嚴以責己，寬以待人，那裏會怨恨別人呢？所以怨恨別人的人，定無學問。

因此，一個人做事處處不能稱心，都是因為自己的道德沒修好，功德沒修滿，感動人的心不夠呀！應該都要反過來自我反省檢討。自己有沒有對不起他人的地方？

能夠這樣的存心用功，那麼別人毀謗我，反而變成磨鍊我，成就我反面的教育場所了。我應該歡歡喜喜地接受別人給我的教訓、批評，還有什麼怨恨呢？

還有，聽到別人說我壞話而能夠不生氣，儘管壞話說得很厲害，像火光薰天，也不過是像拿火去燒空中，虛空中無物可燒；而火卻是終歸要熄滅的。若是聽到別人說壞話，你就生氣；雖然你用盡心思，盡力去辯，結果卻像春天的蠶吐絲，把自己束縛住一樣；這就是所謂的作繭自縛，自討苦吃。所以生氣不但是無益處，並且還是有害的。

這都是說生氣的後果。至於其它種種的過失和罪惡，也都應該依道理，細細去想，像上邊所說的種種道理能夠明白，那就自然而然地不會犯過失了。怎樣叫做從心上改過呢？人的過失，有千千萬萬種那麼多，都是從心上造出來的，我的心不動，就什麼事情都不會造出來，那麼過失還會從何處生出來呢？凡是讀書人，或是喜歡女色，或是喜歡名聲，或是喜歡財物，或是喜歡發火；像這樣種種的過失，不必要一類一類的去

尋求滅過的方法；只要一心一意地發善心，做善事，正的念頭出現在前；那末邪的念頭，自然就污染不上了。

譬如亮熱的太陽當空而照，所有的妖怪，自然會逃避消失了；這就是最精純而唯一的修心補過的真正訣竅啊！須知道過失全部是由這顆心造的，因此也應該由這顆心上來改；正好像斬除毒樹一樣，要斬就斬得乾淨倒落，連根鏟除，才不會再長出來；那又何必要一枝一枝的剪，一葉一葉的摘呢？

改過最上最高的方法，還是修心。能修心，就可使心立刻清淨。因為犯過失，都是心上動了種種壞念頭的緣故。能修心，那末壞念頭一動，就自己發覺。自己能發覺，就立刻把心停住不動；心不動，那麼壞念頭便消失，也就不會再犯了。若是再不能夠這樣，那麼一定要明白，所犯過失的理由，把這種犯過的念頭去掉。若是再不能夠這樣，那麼只好碰到犯過時，

用勉強壓住的方法，來禁止不犯。如果用修心的上等功夫，和明白不可犯過的道理，用打發它去的下等功夫，以及碰到犯過用強壓方法禁止的下等功夫；這上下兩等的功夫，同時用，也不一定就失算呀！若是堅持只用下等功夫，反而把修心的上等功夫忽略不用，那就是最笨不過的了。

但是發願改過，也要有助力；明裏頭，要有眞正的益友在你糊塗的時候時常來提醒你；暗裏頭，要有鬼神替你證明；（像我把自己所犯的過失，做了篇疏文，上告天地鬼神那樣。）還要一心一意的虔誠懺悔，從早到晚，從日到夜，絕不放鬆；像我這樣懺悔經過一個七天，兩個七天；直到一個月，兩個月，三個月．．這樣懺悔下去，一定會有效驗的！

【改過須發，也要有助力，明裡頭，要有益友來提醒呀！來提醒。暗裡頭，要有鬼神做證明呀！做證明。還要一心一意

虔誠的懺悔呀！虔一誠一的一懺一悔。】

　上面所說懺悔過惡的效驗是什麼呢？譬如你或許覺得精神上很舒服，心中很寬閒；或覺得以往很笨，忽然智慧大開。；或是雖然處在煩忙紛亂之際，心中仍清清朗朗，無所不通。；或碰到怨家仇人，而能全把恨心火氣消除，而心生歡喜；或是在夢裏，感覺吐出黑的東西來；這是種種邪念邪思，積成的一種穢氣，夢裏吐出，那麼心地就清淨多了。或是夢到古時候的聖賢來提拔我，牽引我，或是夢見自己會飛到虛空中去，逍遙自在；或是夢見各種彩旗以及裝飾珍寶的傘蓋，這種種少有少見的事情，都是過失消除罪孽滅去的好徵兆。但是也不能因為碰到這些好徵兆。就自己以為了不起，而阻斷了再上進，再努力的途徑。

　從前春秋時代衛國的賢大夫蘧伯玉在二十歲的時候，已經

能時時反醒自己過去的過失，加以檢討，完全改掉了。到了二十一歲的時候，又覺得從前所改的過失，並不徹底；到了二十二歲，再回憶二十一歲時，還像在夢中一般，並不徹底；到了二十的過去，一年一年的逐步改過；直到五十歲那年，還覺得過去的四十九年，都是有過失的。古人對於改過的學問講究就是像這樣的。

【蘧伯玉呀賢大夫，二十歲時就覺悟，時時反省己過失，年年檢討再檢討；總覺得，自己改過工夫不徹底呀，不徹底！所以說，改過的學問須講究呀，須講究！】

我們都是平凡人，過失罪惡，就像刺蝟身上的刺一樣，聚集了滿身都是。而回想過去的事，常常像看不到自己有甚麼過失，這實在都是因為粗心，不知道自我反省。又像眼睛上長了醫，看不到自己天天在那裏犯過呀！但是，一個人的過失，罪

惡深重到了相當的地步，也有證據可以看出來；或者是心思混亂塞住，精神萎靡不振，隨便甚麼事轉頭就忘記了；或者是不值得煩惱的事，也常常感覺非常的煩惱；或者是見到品德高尚的君子，便覺得難為情，垂頭喪氣；或者是聽到光明正大的道理，反倒覺得不歡喜；或者是有恩惠給別人，對方不領情反而怨恨你；或者是夜裏都做些顛顛倒倒的壞夢，甚至語無倫次失掉平常的模樣；像這樣種種不正常的現象，都是作孽的表現啊！

假使你有上邊所說的那種情形，就應該即刻提起精神，奮發向上，把舊的種種過失一齊改掉；而另外開闢一條新的人生大道，希望你千萬不可自己耽誤自己啊！

第三篇　積善之方

上一篇所講，改過的種種方法，能夠把今生的過失改掉，自然好命就不會變成壞命了；但是還不能把壞命變成好命。因為這一生雖然不犯過失造罪孽，卻不知道，若是前世已經犯，但是前世所犯的罪過，還是要受報應。那麼要怎麼樣做才能使壞命轉成好命呢？這不但要改過，還要積善、積德，才可以把前世所造的罪孽消去。善事積多了，自然能轉壞命成好命，並且可以證明它的效驗！

【中國積德第一人，就數山東孔聖人，世代子孫都不衰呀！都不衰，七十三代孔德成呀！孔德成。】

易經上說：積善的家庭，一定會有很多福份喜慶的事。例

如，從前姓嚴的人家，要把他的女兒，配給孔子的父親；就將孔家所作的事情，一件一件都提出來，覺得孔家祖先所積的德，多而且長久；所以預知孔家的子孫，將來必定會大發。後來果然生出了孔子。還有，孔子稱讚舜的孝，是不平凡的孝順，孔子說：像舜這樣的大孝，不但祖先要享受他的祭祀；並且他的世世代代子孫可以保住他的福德，不會敗落。春秋時代的陳國，就是舜傳下來的子孫，足以證明舜的後代興發得相當長久。這都是非常確實的說法啊！

現在我再以過去發生真實的事情，來證明積善的功德。有一位做過少師的人，姓楊名榮，是福建省建寧人。他家世代是以擺渡為生。有一次，雨下得太久，溪水滿漲，水勢洶湧橫衝直撞，把民房都沖失了，被淹死的人順著水勢一直流下來。別的船都去撈取水中漂來的各種財貨，只有少師的曾祖父和祖

父，專門去救水裏漂來的災民，而財物一件都不撈，鄉人都偷笑他們是傻瓜。等到少師的父親出生後，家道也漸漸的寬裕了。有一位神仙化做道士的模樣，向少師的父親說：你的祖父和父親，都積了許多陰功，所生的子孫應該發達做大官。可以將你的父親葬在某一個地方。少師的父親聽了，就照道士所指定的地方，把他的祖父和父親葬下。這座墳，就是現在大家所知道的白兔墳。後來少師出生了，到了二十歲就中了進士。一直做官，做到三公裏面的少師。皇帝還追封他的曾祖父、祖父、父親，與少師一樣的官位。而且少師的後代子孫，都非常興旺，一直到現在還有許多賢能之士。

【楊少師呀！楊少師，祖父曾祖積陰德呀！積陰德；大水來了只救人，財物一概都不取，旁人笑伊是傻瓜，誰知傻瓜享大福呀！享大福！】

浙江寧波人楊自懲，起初在縣衙做書辦，心地非常厚道；而且守法公平，做事公正。；當時的縣官，為人嚴屬方正，有一次偶然打了一個囚犯，一直打到血流到地上，縣官還是不息怒；楊自懲就跪下，替囚犯向縣官求情，請縣官寬諒那個囚犯。縣官說：你求情本來沒有什麼不能放寬的，但是這個囚犯，不守法律，違背道理，不能教人不生氣啊！

楊自懲一邊叩頭一邊說：在朝廷中已經沒有是非可言了，政治一片黑暗、貪污、腐敗，人心散失已經很久了，審問案件若是審出實情，尚且應該替他們傷心，可憐他們不明事理，誤蹈法網，不可以因為審出了案情，就歡喜。若是存心歡喜，恐怕會把案件忽略弄錯。若是生氣，又恐怕犯人受不住打，勉強招認，容易冤枉人。既然歡喜尚且不可，又怎麼可以發火呢？

那縣官聽了楊自懲的話，非常感動，面容立即和緩下來，

不再發怒了！講到楊自懲的家裏，是很窮的；但是他雖然窮，別人送他東西，他一概不肯接受。碰到囚犯缺糧，他卻常用許多方法去弄一些米來，救濟他們。有一天來了幾個新的囚犯，沒有東西吃，非常的餓，他自己家裏剛巧也欠米。若是拿來給囚犯，那麼自己家人就沒得吃了。如果只顧自己吃，那麼囚犯又餓得很可憐，沒有辦法，便同他的妻子商量。他的妻子問他說：犯人從什麼地方來的？從杭州來的。沿途熬餓，臉上餓得沒有一點血色；就像一種又青又黃的菜色，幾乎可以用手捧起來。

因此，兩夫婦就把自己所存的一些米，用來煮稀飯給新來的囚犯吃。然後他們生了兩個兒子，大的叫做守陳，小的叫做守址，作官一直做到南北吏部侍郎。大孫子做到刑部侍郎。小孫子也做到四川按察使。兩個兒子，兩個孫子，都是名臣；而

當今有兩個名人楚亭和德政，都是楊自懲的後代。

【囚犯苦呀！囚犯苦，即坐監牢又挨餓，心中淒苦誰人知呀！誰人知；楊書辦呀心厚道，夫妻同心幫囚犯，積善之家慶有餘呀！慶有餘。】

從前明朝英宗正統年間，有一個土匪首領叫作鄧茂七，在福建一帶造反。福建的讀書人和老百姓，跟隨他一起造反的很多。皇帝就起用曾經擔任都御史的鄞縣人張楷，去搜剿他們。張都憲用計策把鄧茂七捉住了。後來張都憲又派了福建布政司的一位謝都事，去搜查捉拿剩下來的土匪，捉到就殺；但是謝都事不肯亂殺，怕殺錯人。便向各處尋找依附賊黨的名冊，查出來凡是沒有依附賊黨，名冊裏還沒有他們姓名的人。就暗中給他們一面白布小旗，約定他們，搜查賊黨的官兵到的那一天，把這面白布小旗插在自己家門口，表示是清白的民家，並

且禁止官兵不准亂殺。因為有這種措施而避免被殺的人，大約有一萬人之多。後來謝都事的兒子謝遷，就中了狀元，官做到宰相。而且他的孫子謝丕，也中了探花，就是第三名的進士。

【將軍呀，不亂殺，後世子孫一定發呀！一定發！謝都事，心慈悲，全活萬人子孫昌呀！子孫昌！】

在福建省浦田縣的林家，他們的上輩中，有一位老太太喜歡做善事，時常用米粉做粉糰給窮人吃。只要有人向她要，她就立刻給，臉上沒有表現出一點厭煩的樣子。有一位仙人，變作道士，每天早晨向她討六、七個粉糰。老太太每給他，一連三年，每天都是這樣的布施，沒有厭倦過，仙人曉得她作善事的誠心，就向她說：我吃了妳三年的粉糰，要怎樣報答妳呢？這樣吧，妳家後面有一塊地，若是妳死後葬在這塊地上，將來子孫有官爵的，就會像一升麻子那樣的多。

五四

後來老太太去世了，她的兒子依照仙人的指示，把老太太安葬下去。林家的子孫第一代發科甲的，就有九人。後來世世代代，做大官的人非常多。

有姓林的人去赴考，就不能發榜。因此，福建省竟有一句：『如果沒考試的人多，並且都能考中，所以到發榜，榜上就不會沒有姓林的人。表示林家有功名的人很多。』的傳言。意思是講：林家

【林家老太太，喜歡做好事，常常把米粉，做成粉糰送人吃呀，送人吃！佈施心誠懇，神仙也感動，報答老太太，子孫官爵一大堆呀，一大堆！】

馮琢菴太史的父親，當他在縣學裏做秀才的時候，有一個非常寒冷的冬天清早，在要去縣學的路上，碰到一個人倒在雪地裏，用手摸摸看，已經幾乎快要凍死了。馮老先生馬上就把自己穿的皮袍，脫下來替他穿上；並且還扶他到家裏，把他救

醒。馮老先生救人後，就做了一個夢，夢中見到一位天神告訴他說：你救人一命，是完全出自一片至誠的心來救的，所以我要派韓琦投生到你家，做你的兒子。等到後來琢菴生了，就命名叫作馮琦。因爲他是宋朝一個文武全才的賢能宰相，叫作韓琦的人來投胎轉世的。

【馮老爹，心腸好，救人命呀！功德高；誠心誠意救人命，勝過建造七浮屠呀！七浮屠。】

浙江台州有一個應大猷尚書，壯年的時候在山中讀書，夜裡頭，鬼常聚在一起做鬼叫，來嚇唬人，只有應公不怕鬼叫。有一夜，應公聽到一個鬼說：有一個婦人，因爲丈夫出遠門作客，好久沒回來，她的公婆判斷兒子可能已經死了，所以就逼這個婦人改嫁；但是這個婦人卻是要守節，不肯改嫁。所以明天夜裡，她要在這裡上吊，我可以找到一個替身了。凡是上吊

或者是淹死的人，如果沒有替身，便無法投生，所以叫替死鬼。

應公聽到這些話，動了救人的心，偷偷的把自己的田，賣了四兩銀子，還馬上寫了一封假託她丈夫的信；並把銀子寄回家的事寫在信上說明。這位出外人的父母看了信以後，因為筆跡不像，所以懷疑信是假的。但是後來他們又說：信是可以假的，但是銀子不能假呀！一定是兒子很平安，才會把銀子寄回來。

他們這樣想以後，就不再逼媳婦去改嫁了。後來他們的兒子回來了，這對夫婦就得以保全，像從前新婚時一樣，好好的過日子了。隔天晚上，應公又聽到那個鬼說：我本來可以找到替身了，那知被這個秀才壞了我的事啊。

旁邊一個鬼說：喂！你爲什麼不去害死他呢？

那個鬼說：天帝因為這個人心好，有陰德，已經派他去做陰德尚書了，我怎麼還能害他呢？

應公聽了這兩個鬼所講的話以後，就更加努力，更加發心，善事一天一天去做，功德也一天一天的增加；碰到荒年的時候，每次都捐米穀救人；碰到親戚有急難，他一定想盡辦法幫助人家渡過難關；碰到蠻不講理的人，或不如意的事，總會反省，責備自己有過失，就心平氣和地接受事實。因為應公能夠這樣做人，所以他的子孫得到功名，官位的，一直到現在還是很多哩！

【淹死的人呀！吊死的人，都要找替身呀！都要找替身，所以叫做替死鬼呀！替死鬼！】

江蘇省常熟縣有一位徐鳳竹先生，他的父親本來就很富有。偶然碰到了荒年，就先把他應收的田租，完全捐掉，做為

全縣有田的人的榜樣。同時又分他自己原有的稻穀，去救濟窮人。有一天夜裡，他聽到有一群鬼在門口唱道：千也不說謊，萬也不說謊，徐家秀才，快要做到了舉人！

【千也不說謊，萬也不說謊，徐家的秀才，快做舉人郎呀！快做舉人郎。】

那些鬼連續不斷的呼叫，夜夜不停。這一年，徐鳳竹去參加鄉試，果然考中了舉人。他的父親因此更加高興，努力不倦地做善事，積功德；同時又修橋鋪路，施齋飯供養出家人；碰到缺米缺衣的人，也接濟他們；凡是對別人有好處的事情，無不盡心的去做。後來他又聽到鬼在門前唱道：千也不說謊，萬也不說謊，徐家舉人，做官直做到都堂！結果徐鳳竹，官做到了兩浙的巡撫。【千也不說謊，萬也不說謊，徐家的舉人，官做到都堂呀！官做到都堂。】

浙江省嘉興縣有一位姓屠，名叫康僖的人，起初在刑部

裏做主事的官，夜裏就住在監獄裡。並且仔細的盤問囚犯，結

果發現沒罪而被冤枉的，有不少人；但是屠公並不覺得自己有

功勞，他祕密地把這件事，上公文告訴了刑部堂官。

後來到了秋審的時候，刑部堂官，把屠公所提供的話，揀

些要點，來審問那些囚犯。囚犯們都老老實實的向堂官供認，

沒有一個不心服的。因此，堂官就把原來冤枉的，因為受刑不

住被逼招認的，釋放了十多人。

那個時候京裡的百姓，都稱讚刑部尚書明察秋毫。後來屠

公又向堂官上了一份公文說：在天子腳下，尚且有那麼多被冤

枉的人；那麼全國這樣大的地方，千千萬萬的百姓，那會沒有

被冤枉的人呢？所以應該每五年再派一位減刑官，到各省去細

查因犯犯罪的實情，確實有罪的，定罪也要公平；若是冤枉

了凡四訓白話篇

六〇

的，應該翻案重審，減輕或者釋放。

尚書就代爲上奏皇帝，皇帝也准了他所建議的辦法；就派

減刑官，到各省去查察，剛巧屠公也派在內。有一天晚上屠公

夢見天神告訴他說：你命裡本來沒有兒子，但是因爲你提出減

刑的建議，正與天心相合；所以上帝賜給你三個兒子，將來都

可以做大官；穿紫色的袍，束金鑲的帶。這天晚上，屠公的夫

人就有了身孕；後來生下了應塤、應坤、應竣三個兒子，果然

都作了高官。

【屠康僖呀！屠康僖，辦刑案，有一套，明察秋毫不貪

功，平反冤案十多起，建議減刑合天心，命裡無子得三子，個

個都是做高官呀！做高官。】

有一位嘉興人，姓包，名叫憑，號信之。他的父親做過安

徽池州府的太守。生了七個兒子，包憑是最小的。他被平湖縣

姓袁的人家，招贅做女婿；和我父親常常來往，交情很深。他的學問廣博，才氣很高，但是每次考試都考不中。因此他對佛教、道教的學問，很注意研究。

有一天，他向東去卯湖遊玩，偶然到了一處鄉村的佛寺裏，因為寺內房屋壞了，看見觀世音菩薩的聖像，露天而立，被雨淋得很濕。當時就打開他的袋子，有十兩銀子，就拿給這寺裏的住持和尚，叫他修理寺院房屋。和尚告訴他說：修寺的工程大，銀子少，不夠用，沒法完工。

因此，他又拿了松江出產的布四匹，再撿竹箱裏的七件衣服給和尚。這七件衣服裏，有用麻織的料做的夾衣，是新做的；他的佣人要他不要再送了，但是包憑說：只要觀世音菩薩的聖像，能夠安好，不被雨淋，我就是赤身露體又有甚麼關係呢？和尚聽後流著眼淚說：施送銀兩和衣服布四，還不是件難

了凡四訓白話篇

六二

事，只是這一點誠心，怎麼容易得到呀！

後來房屋修好了，包憑就拉著他父親同遊這座佛寺，並且住在寺中。那天晚上，包憑做了一個夢，夢到寺裏的護法神，來謝他說：你做了這些功德，你的兒子可以世世代代享受官祿了。後來他的兒子包汴，孫子包檉芳，都中了進士，做到高官。

【包信之，學問好，才氣高，可惜考試都不中；偶到一處鄉村裡，見佛寺、觀音像，風吹雨打露天立，佈施心、油然生，難捨能捨心虔誠，感動得和尚流眼淚，夢裡護法來道謝，兒孫世世受官祿呀！受官祿。】

浙江省嘉善縣有一個叫做支立的人，他的父親，在縣衙中的刑房當書辦。有一個囚犯，因為被人冤枉陷害，判了死罪；支書辦很可憐他，想要替他向上面的長官求情，寬免他不死。

那個囚犯曉得支書辦的好意之後，告訴他的妻子說：支公的好意，我覺得很慚愧，沒法子報答；明天請他到鄉下來，妳就嫁給他，他或者會感念這份情份，那麼我就可能有活命的機會了。

他的妻子聽了之後，沒別的辦法，所以就邊哭邊答應了。到了明天，支書辦到了鄉下，囚犯的妻子就自己出來勸支書辦喝酒，並且把他丈夫的意思，完全告訴了支書辦。但是支書辦不願意這樣做，不過究竟還是盡了全力替這個囚犯，把案子平反了。後來，囚犯出獄，夫妻兩個人一起到支書辦家裡叩頭拜謝說：您這樣厚德的人，在近代實在是少有。現在您沒有兒子，我有一個女兒，願意送給您做掃地的小妾。這在情理上是可以說得通的。

支書辦聽了他的話，就預備了禮物，把這個囚犯的女兒迎

娶為妾，後來生了一個兒子叫支立，才二十歲就中了舉人的前茅，官做到翰林院的書記，後來支立的兒子叫做支高，支高的兒子叫支祿，都被保薦做州學縣裡的教官。而支祿的兒子叫支大綸，也考中了進士。

【支書辦，刑房吏，有位囚犯遭冤屈，被判死罪真可憐；支書辦，心慈悲，平反冤獄無條件，厚德感動死囚犯呀！死囚犯！】

以上這十條故事，雖然每人所做的各不相同，不過行的都是一個善字罷了。若是要再精細的加以分類來說，那末做善事；有真的，有假的；有直的，有曲的；有陰的，有陽的；有是的，有不是的；有偏的，有正的；有一半的，有圓滿的；有大的，有小的；有難的，有易的；

這種種都各有各的道理，都應該要仔細的辨別。若是做善

事，而不知道考究做善事的道理，就自誇自己做善事，做得怎樣有功德，那裏知道這不是在做善事，而是在造孽。這樣做豈不是冤枉，白費苦心，得不到一些益處啊！我現在把上面所說過的，分類來加以說明。怎麼叫做真假呢？從前在元朝的時候

有幾個讀書人，去拜見天目山的高僧中峰和尚，問說：佛家講善惡的報應，像影子跟著身體一樣，人到那裏，影子也到那裏，永遠不分離。這是說行善，定有好報，造惡定有苦報，決不會不報的。為什麼現在某一個人是行善的，他的子孫反而不興旺？有某一個人是作惡的，他的家反倒發達得很？那末佛說的報應，倒是沒有憑據了。

中峰和尚回答說：平常人被世俗的見解所蒙蔽，這顆靈明的心，沒有洗除乾淨，因此，法眼未開，所以把真的善行反認為是惡的，真的惡行反算它是善的，這是常有的事情；並且看

錯了，還不恨自己顛顛倒倒，怎麼反而抱怨天的報應錯了呢？

大家又說：善就是善，惡就是惡，善惡那裡會弄得相反呢？

中峰和尚聽了之後，便叫他們把所認為是善的，惡的事情都說出來。其中有一個人說：罵人，打人是惡；恭敬人，用禮貌待人是善。

中峰和尚說：你說的也不一定是對喔！

另外一個讀書人說：貪財，亂要錢是惡；不貪財，清清白白守正道，是善。

中峰和尚回答說：你說的不一定對喔！

那些讀書人，都把各人平時所看到的種種善惡的行為都講出來，但是中峰和尚都說：不一定全對喔！

那幾個讀書人，因為他們所說的善惡，中峰和尚都說他們說得不對，所以就請問和尚，究竟怎樣才是善？怎樣才是惡？

中峰和尚告訴他們說：做對別人有益的事情，是善；做對自己有益的事情，是惡。若是做的事情，可以使別人得到益處，那怕是罵人，打人，也都是善；而有益於自己的事情，那麼就是恭敬人，用禮貌待人，也都是惡。所以一個人做的善事，使旁人得到利益的就是公，公就是真了；只想到自己要得到的利益，就是私，私就是假了。並且從良心上所發出來的善行，是真；只不過是照例做做就算了的，是假。還有，為善不求報答，不露痕跡，那麼所做的善事，是真；但是為著某一種目的，企圖有所得，才去做的善事，是假；像這樣的種種，自己都要仔細地考察。

怎樣叫做端曲呢？現在的人，看見謹慎不倔強的人，大都稱他是善人，而且很看重他；然而古時的聖賢，卻是寧願欣賞志氣高，只向前進的人，或者是安份守己，不肯亂來的人。因

為這種人，才有擔當，有作為，可以教導他，使他上進。

至於那些看起來謹慎小心卻是無用的好人，雖然在鄉里，大家都喜歡他；但是因為這種人的個性軟弱，隨波逐流，沒有志氣，所以聖人一定要說這種人，是傷害道德的賊。這樣看來，世俗人所說的善惡觀念，分明是和聖人相反。

俗人說是善的，聖人反而說是惡；俗人說是惡的，聖人反而說是善。從這一個觀念，推廣到各種不同的事情來說，俗人所喜歡的，或者是不喜歡的，完全不同於聖人。那還有不錯的嗎？天地鬼神庇佑善人報應惡人，他們都和聖人的看法是一樣的，聖賢以為是對的，天地鬼神也以為是對的；聖賢以為是錯的，天地鬼神也認為是錯的，而不和世俗人採取相同的看法。所以凡要積功德，絕對不可以被耳朵所喜歡的聲音，眼睛所喜歡的景象所利用，而跟著感覺在走；必須要從起心動念隱微的

地方，將自己的心，默默地洗滌清淨，不可讓邪惡的念頭，污染了自己的心。

所以全是救濟世人的心，是直；如果存有一些討好世俗的心，就是曲。全是愛人的心，是直；如果有一絲一毫對世人怨恨不平的心，就是曲；全是恭敬別人的心，就是直；如果有一絲玩弄世人的心，就是曲。這些都應該細細的去分辨。

怎樣叫做陰陽呢？凡是一個人做善事被人知道，叫做陽善；做善事而別人不知道，叫做陰德。有陰德的人，上天自然會知道並且會報酬他的。有陽善的人，大家都曉得他，稱讚他，他便享受世上的美名。享受好名聲，雖然也是福，但是名這個東西，為天地所忌，天地是不喜歡愛名之人的。只要看世界上享受極大名聲的人，而他實際上沒有功德，可以稱配他所享受的名聲，常會遭遇到料想不到的橫禍，一個人並沒有過失

差錯，反倒被冤枉，無緣無故被人栽上一惡名的人，他的子孫，常常會忽然間發達起來。這樣看來，陰德和陽善的分別，真是細微得很，不可以不加以分辨啊！

怎樣叫做是非呢？從前春秋時代的魯國定有一種法律，凡是魯國人被別的國家抓去做奴隸；若有人肯出錢，把這些人贖回來，就可以向官府領取賞金。但是孔子的學生子貢，他很有錢，雖然也替人贖回被抓去的人回來，子貢卻是不肯接受魯國的賞金。他不肯接受賞金，純粹是幫助他人，本意是很好。但是孔子聽到之後，很不高興的説：這件事子貢做錯了，凡是聖賢無論做什麼事情，都是要做了以後，能把風俗變好；可以教訓，引導百姓做好人，這種事才可以做；不是單單為了自己覺得爽快稱心，就去做的。現在魯國富有的人少，窮苦的人多；若是受了賞金就算是貪財；那末不肯受貪財之名的人，和錢不

多的人，就不肯去贖人了。一定要很有錢的人，才會去贖人。

如果這樣的話，恐怕從此以後，就不會再有人向諸侯贖人了。

子路看見一個人，跌在水裏，把他救了上來。那個人就送

一隻牛來答謝子路，子路就接受了。孔子知道了，很欣慰的

說：從今以後，魯國就會有很多人，自動到深水大河中去救人

了。

七二

由這兩件事，用世俗的眼光來看，子貢不接受賞金是好

的，子路接受牛，是不好的；不料孔子反而稱讚子路，責備子

貢。照這樣看來，要知道一個人做善事，不能只看眼前的效

果，而要講究是不是會產生流傳下去的弊端；不能只論一時的

影響，而是要講究長遠的是非；不能只論個人的得失，而是要

講究它關係天下大眾的影響。

現在所爲，雖然是善，但是如果流傳下去，對人有害，那

就雖然像善，實在還不是善；現在所行，雖然不是善，但是如果流傳下去，能夠幫助人，那就雖然像不善，實在倒是善！這只不過是拿一件事情來講講罷了。說到其它種種，實在倒有很多。

例如：一個人應該做的事情，叫做義，但是有的時候，做該做的事，也會做錯，做了倒反壞事。

譬如壞人，可以不必寬放他，有人寬放他，這事情不能說不是義；但是寬放了這個壞人，反而使他的膽子更大，壞事做得更多；結果旁人受害，自己也犯罪；倒不如不要寬放他，給他做戒，使他不再犯罪的好，不寬放他，是非義，使這個人不再犯罪，是義，這就叫做非義之義。

禮貌是人人應該有的，但是要有分寸，用禮貌對待人，是禮；但若是過份，反而使人驕傲起來，就成為非禮了，這就叫做非禮之禮。

信；要顧全小信，卻誤了大事；反而使得大信，不能顧全，就

變成非信了，這就叫做非信之信。

信用雖要緊，但是也要看狀況，譬如：顧全小的信用，是

愛人本來是慈；但是因為過份的慈愛，反而使人膽子變

大，闖出大禍，那就變成不慈了，這就叫做非慈之慈。這些問

題，都應該細細地加以判斷，分別清楚。

什麼叫做偏正呢？從前明朝的宰相呂文懿公剛才辭掉宰相

的官位，回到家鄉來，因為他做官清廉，公正，全國的人都敬

佩他，就像是群山拱衛著泰山，眾星環繞著北斗星一樣。獨獨

有一個鄉下人，喝醉酒後，罵呂公。但是呂公並沒有因為被他

罵而生氣，並向自己的用人說：這個人喝酒醉了，不要和他計

較。

呂公就關了門，不理睬他。過了一年，這個人犯了死罪入

獄，呂公方才懊悔的講：若是當時同他計較，將他送到官府治罪，可以藉小懲罰而收到大懲戒的效果，他就不至於犯下死罪了，我當時只想心存厚道，所以就輕輕放過他；那知道，反而養成他天不怕地不怕的亡命之徒的惡性。他以爲就算是罵宰相，也沒什麼大不了，一直到犯下死罪，送了性命。這就是存善心，反倒做了惡事的一個例子。

也有存了惡心，倒反而做了善事的例子。像有一個大富人家，碰到荒年，窮人大白天在市場上搶米；這個大富人家，便告到縣官那裏；縣官偏偏又不受理這個案子，窮人因此膽子更大，愈加放肆橫行了。於是這個大富人家就私底下把搶米的人捉起來關，出他的醜，那些搶米的人，怕這大富人家捉人，反倒安定下來，不再搶了。若不是因爲這樣，市面上幾乎大亂了。所以善是正，惡是偏，這是大家都知道的。但是也有存善

心，反倒做了惡事的例子。

這是存心雖正，結果變成偏，只可稱做正中的偏；不過也有存惡心，反倒做了善事的例子，這是存心雖是偏，結果反成正，只可稱做偏中的正；這種道理大家不可不知道。怎樣叫做半滿的善呢？易經上說：一個人不積善，不會成就好的名譽；不積惡，則不會有殺身的大禍。

書經上說：商朝的罪孽，像穿的一串錢那麼滿；就彷彿收藏東西裝滿了一個容器裏一樣。

如果你很勤奮的，天天去儲積，那麼終有一天就會積滿。商朝由開國一直到紂王，它的過失罪惡，到此時便積滿了，因此迅速亡國。如果懶惰些，不去收藏積存，那就不會滿。所說的積善積惡，也像儲存東西一樣，這是講半善滿善的一種說法。

從前有一戶人家的女子，到佛寺裡去，想要送些錢給寺裡，可惜身上沒有多的錢，只有兩文錢，就拿來布施給和尚。

而寺裡的首席和尚，竟然親自替她在佛前迴向，求懺悔滅罪。

後來這位女子進了皇宮做了貴妃，富貴之後，便帶了幾千兩的銀子來寺裡布施。但是這位主僧，卻只是叫他的徒弟，替那個女子迴向罷了。

那個女子不懂前後兩次的布施，為什麼待遇差別如此之大？就問主僧說：我從前不過布施兩文錢，師父就親自替我懺悔。現在我布施了幾千兩銀子，而師父不替我迴向，不知是什麼道理？

主僧回答她說：從前布施的銀子雖然少，但是你布施的心，很真切虔誠，所以非我老和尚親自替你懺悔，便不足以報答你布施的功德；現在布施的錢雖然多，但是你布施的心，不像從前真切，所以叫人代你懺悔，也就夠了。這就是幾千兩銀

子的布施，只算是半善；而兩文錢的布施，卻算是滿善，道理在此。

又漢朝人鍾離把他煉丹的方法，傳給呂洞賓，用丹點在鐵上，就能變成黃金，可拿來救濟世上的窮人。呂洞賓問鍾離說：變了金，到底會不會再變回鐵呢？

鍾離回答說：五百年以後，仍舊要變回原來的鐵。

呂洞賓又說：像這樣就會害了五百年以後的人，我不願意做這樣的事情。

鍾離教呂洞賓點鐵成金，不過是試試他的心而已。現在知道呂洞賓存心善良，所以對他說：修仙要積滿三千件功德，聽你這句話，你的三千件功德，已經做圓滿了。

這是半善滿善的又一種講法。一個人做善事，而內心不可叨念，彷彿自己做了一件不得了的善事；能夠這樣，那麼就隨

便你所做的任何善事，都能夠成功而且圓滿。若是做了件事，這個心就牢記在這件善事上；雖然一生都很勤勉的做善事，也只不過是半善而已。

譬如拿錢去救濟人，要內不見布施的我，外不見受布施的人，中不見布施的錢，這纔叫做三輪體空，也叫做一心清淨。如果能夠這樣的布施，縱使布施不過一斗米，也可以種下無邊無涯的福了；即使布施一文錢，也可以消除一千劫所造的罪了。如果這個心，不能夠忘掉所做的善事；雖然用了二十萬兩黃金去救濟別人，還是不能夠得到圓滿的福。這又是一種說法。

怎麼叫做大善小善呢？從前有一個人，叫做衛仲達，在翰林院裏做官，有一次被鬼卒把他的魂引到了陰間。陰間的主審判官，吩咐手下的書辦，把他在陽間所做的善事、惡事兩種冊

子送上來。等冊子送到一看，他的惡事冊子，多得竟攤滿了一

院子；而善事的冊子，只不過像一支筷子那樣小罷了。主審官又吩咐拿秤來秤秤看，那攤滿院子的惡冊子反而比較輕，而像一支筷子那樣小捲的善冊子反而比較重。衛仲達就問說：我年紀還不到四十歲，那會犯了這麼多的過失罪惡呢？

主審官說：只要一個念頭，動了壞念頭，那就是犯過。不必等到你去犯，譬如看見女色，動了壞念頭，那就是罪惡。

因此，衛仲達就問這善冊子裡記的是什麼。主審官說：皇帝有一次曾想要興建大工程，修三山地方的石橋。你上奏勸皇帝不要修，免得勞民傷財，這就是你的奏章底稿。

衛仲達說：我雖然講過，但是皇帝不聽，還是動工了，對那件事情的進行，並沒有發生作用，這份疏表怎麼還能有這樣大的力量呢？

八〇

主審官說：皇帝雖然沒有聽你的建議，但是你這個念頭，目的是要使千萬百姓免去勞役；倘使皇帝聽你的，那善的力量就更大了哩！

所以立志做善事，目的在利益天下國家百姓，那麼善事縱然小，功德卻很大。假使只為了利益自己一個人，那麼善事雖然多，功德卻很小。

怎麼叫做難行易行的善呢？從前有學問的讀書人，都說：克制自己的私欲，要從難除去的地方先除起。

孔子的弟子樊遲，問孔子怎樣叫作仁？孔子也說，先要從難的地方下工夫。

孔子所說的難，也就是除掉私心；並應該先從最難做，最難克除的地方做起。一定要像江西的一位舒老先生，他在別人家教書，把兩年所僅得的薪水，幫助一戶窮人，還了他們所欠

公家的錢，而免除他們夫婦被拆散的悲劇。

又像河北邯鄲縣的張老先生，看到一個窮人，把妻兒抵押了，錢也用了；若是沒有錢去贖回，恐怕妻兒都要活不成了。於是就捨棄他十年的積蓄，替這個窮人贖回他的妻兒。像舒老先生，張老先生，都是在最難處，旁人不容易捨的，他們竟然能夠捨得啊！

又像江蘇省鎮江的一位靳老先生，雖然年老沒有兒子，他的窮鄰居，願意把一個年輕的女兒給他做妾，願能為他生一個兒子。但是這位靳老先生不忍心誤了她的青春，還是拒絕了，就把這女子送還鄰居。這又是很難忍處，而能夠忍得住的事呀！所以上天賜給他們這幾位老先生的福，也特別的豐厚。

【善有真，也有假，有端有曲有陰陽，有是有非有偏正，有半有滿有大小，有難有易當深辨呀，當深辨！】

凡是有財有勢的人要立些功德，比平常人來得容易，但是容易做，卻不肯做，那就叫做自暴自棄了；而沒錢沒勢的窮人，要做些福，都會有很大的困難，難做到而能做到，這才真是可貴啊！我們為人處事，應該遇到機緣，就去做救濟眾人的事。不過救濟眾人，也不是容易的事，救濟眾人的種類很多，簡單的說，它的重要項目，大約有十種：

第一、是與人為善。看到別人有一點善心，我就幫他，使他善心增長。別人做善事，力量不夠，做不成功，我就幫他，使他做成功，這都是與人為善。

第二、是愛敬存心。就是對比我學問好，年紀大，輩份高的人，都應該心存敬重。而對比我年紀小，輩份低，景況窮的人，都該要心存愛護。

第三、是成人之美。譬如一個人，要做件好事，尚未決

定，則應該勸他盡心盡力去做。別人做善事時，遇到了阻礙；

不能成功，應想方法，指引他，勸導他使得他成功；而不可生

嫉妒心去破壞他。

第四、是勸人為善。碰到做惡的人，要勸他做惡絕對有苦

報，惡事萬萬做不得。碰到不肯為善，或只肯做些小善的人，

就要勸他行善絕對有好報，善事不但要做，而且還要做得多。

做得大。

第五、是救人危急。一般人大多喜歡錦上添花，而缺乏雪

中送炭的精神；而當遇到他人最危險、最困難、最緊急的關

頭；能及時向他伸出援手，拉他一把，出錢出力幫他解決危急

困境，可以說是功德無量，但是不可以引以為傲！

第六、是興建大利。有大利益的事情，自然要有大力量的

人，才能做到，一個人既然有大力量，自然應該做些大利益的

事情，以利益大眾。例如，修築水利系統、救濟大災害等等。但是沒有大力量的人，也可以做到的。譬如，發現河堤上有個小洞，水從洞裡冒出，只要用些泥土、小石，將小洞塞住，這堤防就可以保住，而防止了水災的發生。事情雖然小，但這種功效也是不可忽視的。

第七、是捨財作福。俗語說：人為財死，世人的心總愛錢財，求財都來不及，還願意去捨財濟助他人嗎？因此，能捨財去消除別人的災難，解決他人的危急；對一個常人而言，已不簡單，對窮人來說，則更加了不起。如按因果來講，「捨得，捨得，有捨才有得。」「捨不得，捨不得，不捨就不得。」；做一分善事就會有一分福報，所以不必憂愁我們會因為捨財救人，而使自己的生活陷於絕路。

第八、是護持正法。這種法，就是指各種宗教的法。宗教

有正，有邪，法也有正，有邪，邪教的邪法最害人心，自然應該禁止。而具有正知正見的佛法，是最容易勸導人心，挽回善良風俗的。若是有人破壞，一定要用全力保護維持，不可讓他破壞。

第九、是敬重尊長。凡是學問深，見識好，職位高，輩份大，年紀老的人，都稱為尊長。自己都應該敬重，不可看輕他們。

第十、是愛惜物命。凡是有性命的東西，雖然像螞蟻那樣小；也是有知覺的，曉得痛苦，並且也會貪生怕死。應該要哀憐它們，怎可以亂殺亂吃呢？有人常說：這些東西，本來就是要給人吃的。這話是最不通的，而且都是貪吃的人所造出來的話。

以上所講的十種，只是大概的說明，下面是分別舉例比

喻：什麼叫做與人善呢？從前虞朝的舜，在他還沒有做君主之前，在雷澤湖邊看見年輕力壯的漁夫，都揀湖水深處去抓魚；而那些年老體弱的漁夫，都在水流得急而且水較淺的地方抓。水流急，魚停不住，淺灘水少，魚也比較少，不比水深的地方，魚都在那裡游來游去，較容易抓。那些年輕力壯的漁夫，把好的地方都佔去了。

舜看見這種情形，心裡面悲傷哀憐他們。就想了一個方法，他自己也去參加捉魚，看見那些喜歡搶奪的人，就把他們的過失，掩蓋起來，而且也不對外講；看見那些比較謙讓的漁夫，便到處稱讚他們，拿他們作榜樣，並且學習他們謙讓的模樣。像這樣，舜抓了一年的魚，大家都把水深魚多的地方讓出來了。

舜的故事，不過是用來勸化人，不可誤解是勸人抓魚。要

知道抓魚是犯殺生的罪孽，千萬不可以做啊！那麼像舜那樣明白聰明的聖人，那有不能說幾句中肯的話，來教化眾人，而是拿自己定要親自參與呢？要曉得舜不用言語來教化眾人，而是拿自己做榜樣，使人見了，感覺慚愧而改變自己的自私心理，這真是一個用心良苦的人，所費的苦心啊！

我們生在這個人心風俗敗壞，末世的時代，做人很不容易；因此，旁人有不如我的地方，不可以把自己的長處，去蓋過旁人。旁人有不善的事情，不可以把自己的善，來和別人比較。別人能力不及我，不可以把自己有的能力，來為難別人。自己縱然有才幹聰明，也要收斂起來，不可以外露炫耀，應該像是沒有聰明才幹一樣。要看聰明才幹，都是虛的、假的一般。

看到別人有過失，姑且替他包含掩蓋。像這樣，一方面可

了凡四訓白話篇

八八

以使他有改過自新的機會，另一方面可以使他有所顧忌而不敢放肆。若是扯破面皮，他就沒有顧忌了。

看到旁人有些小的長處，可以學的，或有小的善心善事，可以記的；都應該立刻翻轉過來，放下自己的主見，學他的長處；並且稱讚他，替他廣為傳揚。一個人在平常生活中，不論講句話或是做件事，全不可為自己，發起一種自私自利的念頭；而要全為了社會大眾設想，立出一種規則來，使大眾可以通行遵守，這才是一位偉大的人物，把天下所有的一切，都看做是公而不是私的度量呢！

什麼叫做愛敬存心呢？君子與小人，從外貌來看，常常容易混淆，分不出真假。因為小人會裝假仁假義，冒充君子。不過這一點存心，君子是善，小人是惡，彼此相去很遠，他們的分別，就像黑白兩種顏色，絕對相反不同。所以孟子說：君子

所以與常人不同的地方，就是他們的存心啊！君子所存的心，只有愛人敬人的心。因為人雖然有親近的，疏遠的，有尊貴的，有低微的，有聰明的，有愚笨的，有道德的，有下流的，千千萬萬不同的種類；但是這些都是我們的同胞，都是和我們一樣有生命，有血有肉，有感情，那一個不該愛他敬他呢？愛敬眾人，就是愛敬聖賢人的意思，就是明白聖賢人的意思。為什麼呢？

因為聖賢人本來都希望世界上的人，大家都能安居樂業，過著幸福美滿的生活。所以，我們能夠處處愛人，處處敬人，使世上的人，個個平安幸福，也就可以說是代替聖賢，使這個世界上人人都能夠平安快樂了。

什麼叫做成人之美呢？舉例來說，若是把一塊裏面有玉的石頭，隨便亂丟拋棄，那末這塊裏面有玉的石頭也只不過是和

瓦片碎石一樣，一文不值了。若是把它好好的加以雕刻琢磨，那麼這塊石頭，就成了非常珍貴的寶物主璋了。

一個人也是如此，也全是靠勸導提引；所以看到別人做一件善事，或者是這個人立志向上，而且他的資質足以造就的話；都應該好好的引導他，使他成為社會上的有用之材；或是誇讚他，激勵他，扶持他；若是有人冤枉他，就替他辯解冤屈，來替他分擔無端被人惡意的毀謗，可以設法代替他，頂替他被毀謗的事實，減輕他所受的毀謗，這樣叫做分謗。

務必要使他能夠立身於社會，而後才算是盡了我的心意。

大概通常的人，對那些與他不同類型的人，都不免有厭惡感，譬如小人恨君子，惡人恨善人。

在同一個鄉里的人，都是善的少，不善的多。正因為不善

的人很多，善的人少，所以善人處在世俗裡，常常被惡人欺負，很難立得住腳，況且豪傑的性情大多數是剛正不屈，並且不注意修飾外表，世俗的眼光，見識不高，只看外表，就說長道短，隨便批評；所以做善事也常常容易失敗，善人也常常被人毀謗。

碰到這種情形，只有全靠仁人長者，才能糾正那些邪惡不正的人，教導指引他們改邪歸正，保護，幫助善人，使他成立；像這樣闢邪顯正的功德，實在是最大的。

什麼叫做勸人為善呢？一個人既然已經生在世上做了人，那一個沒有良心呢？但是因為汲汲地追逐名利，弄得這世間忙碌不堪，只要有名利可得，就昧著良心，不擇手段地去做，那就最容易墮落了。所以與別人往來相處，時常要留心觀察這個人，若是看他要墮落了，就應該隨時隨地提醒他，警告他，開

發他的糊塗昏亂。

譬如，看見他在長夜裡做了一個渾渾噩噩的夢，一定要叫喚他，使他趕快清醒；又譬如看他長久陷落在煩惱裡，一定要提拔他一把，使他頭腦轉為清涼。

像這樣以恩待人，功德是最周遍，最廣大的了。從前韓文公曾說：以口來勸人，只在一時，事情過了，也就忘了；並且別處的人，無法聽到。以書來勸人，可以流傳到百世，並且能傳遍世界；所以做善書，有立言的大功德。

這裡說以口來勸，用書來勸人為善，與前面所講的與人為善比較起來，雖然較注重形式的痕跡，但是這種對症下藥的事，時常會有特殊的效果；這種方法是不可以放棄的。

並且勸人也得要勸的得當，譬如這個人太倔強，不可以用話來勸，你若是用話去勸了，不但是白勸，所勸的話，也成了

廢話，這叫做失言。如果這個人性情溫順，可以用話來勸，你卻是不勸，錯過了勸人爲善的機會，這叫做失人。失言失人，都是自己智慧不夠，分辨不出來，就應該自己仔細反省檢討；如此才能不失言，也不失人。

什麼叫做救人危急呢？患難顚沛的事情，在人的一生當中，都是常有的。假使偶而碰到患難危急的人，應該要將他的痛苦，當做是發生在自己的身上一樣，趕快設法解救，看他有什麼被人冤屈壓迫的事情，或是用話語幫助他申辯明白，或是用種種的方法來救濟他的困苦。明朝的崔子曾經說：恩惠不在乎大小，只要在別人危急的時候，趕緊去幫助他就可以了。這句話眞正是仁者的話呀！

什麼叫做興建大利呢？講小的，在一個鄉中，講大的，在一個縣內，凡是有益公眾的事，最應該發起興建。或是開闢水

道來灌溉農田；或是建築堤岸來預防水災；或是修築橋樑，使行旅交通方便，或是施送茶飯，救濟飢餓口渴的人。

隨時遇到機會，都要勸導大家，同心協力，出錢出力來興建；縱然有別人在暗中毀謗你，中傷你；你也不要為了避嫌疑就不去做，也不要怕辛苦，擔心別人嫉妒怨恨，就推託不做，這都是不可以的。

什麼叫做捨財作福呢？佛們裡的萬種善行，以布施為最重要。講到布施，就只有一個捨字，什麼都捨得，就合佛的意思了。

真正明白道理的人，什麼都肯捨；譬如自己身上的眼睛，耳朵，鼻子，舌頭，身體，念頭，沒有一樣不肯捨掉。譬如，佛陀曾在因地修行的時候，捨身飼虎。

在身外的色、聲、香、味、觸、法，也都可以一概捨棄。

一個人所有的一切，沒有一樣不可以捨掉，能夠如此，那就身心清淨，沒有煩惱，就如同佛菩薩了。

若是不能什麼都捨，那就先從錢財上著手布施。世間人都把穿衣吃飯，看得像生命一樣重要；因此，錢財上的布施也最為重要；如果我能夠痛痛快快地施捨錢財；對內而言，可以破除我小器的毛病；對外而言，則可救濟別人的急難。

不過錢財不易看破，起初做起來，難免會有一些勉強，只要捨慣了，心中自然安逸，也就沒有什麼捨不得了。這是最容易消除自己的貪念私心，也可以除掉自己對錢財的執著與吝嗇。

什麼叫做護持正法呢？法是千萬年來，有靈性的有情生命的眼目，也是真理的準繩；但是法有正有邪，如果沒有正法，如何能夠參加幫助天地造化之功呢？怎樣會使得各式各樣的人

以及種種的東西，都能夠像裁布成衣那樣的成功呢？怎樣可以脫出那種種的迷惑，離開那種種的束縛呢？怎樣可以建設整理世上一切的事情，和逃出這個污穢世界，生死輪迴的苦海呢？這都需要靠有了正法，纔像有了光明的大路可走。

所以凡是看到聖賢的寺廟，圖像，經典，遺訓，都要加以敬重；至於有破損不完全的，都應該要修補，整理。而講到佛門正法，尤其應該敬重的加以傳播宣揚，使大家都重視，纔可以上報佛的恩德，這些都是更應該加以全力去實踐的。

什麼叫做敬重尊長呢？家裏的父親，兄長，國家的君王，長官；以及凡是年歲，道德，職位，見識高的人，都應該格外虔誠的去敬重他們。

在家裡侍奉父母，要有深愛父母的心，與委婉和順的容貌；而且聲要和，氣要平；這樣不斷地薰染成習慣，就變成自

然的好性情，這就是和氣可以感動天心的根本辦法。

出門在外侍候君王，不論什麼事，都應該依照國法去做；不可以為君王不知道，自己就可以隨意亂做呀！辦一個犯罪的人，不論他的罪輕或重，都要仔細審問，公平地執法；不可以為君王不知道，就可以作威作福冤枉人！

服侍君王，像面對上天一樣的恭敬，這是古人所訂的規範，這種地方關係陰德最大。你們試看，凡是忠孝人家，他們的子孫，沒有不發達久遠而且前途興旺的，所以一定要小心謹慎的去做。

什麼叫做愛惜物命呢？要知道一個人之所以能夠算他是人，就是在他有這一片惻隱的心罷了。所以孟子說：沒有惻隱之心就不是人。

求仁的，就是求這一片惻隱之心；積德的，也就是積這一

了凡四訓白話篇

九八

片惻隱的心。有惻隱心就是仁；有惻隱心，就是德。沒有惻隱

心，就是無仁心，沒道德。周禮上曾說：每年正月的時候，正

是畜牲最容易懷孕的期間，這時候祭品勿用母的。因為要預防

畜牲肚裡有胎兒的緣故。

孟子說：君子不肯住在廚房附近。就是要保全自己的惻隱

之心，所以，前輩有四種肉不吃的禁忌。譬如說，聽到動物被

殺的聲音，不吃，或者在它被殺的時候看見，不吃；或者是自

己養大的，不吃，或專門為我殺的，不吃。後輩的人，若要學

習前輩的仁慈心，一下子做不到斷食葷腥，也應該依照前輩的

辦法，禁戒少吃。

照佛法來講，一切有生命的東西，都是因為前生造了孽而

投胎做畜牲；等到它們的罪孽還完了後，仍然可以投胎做人

的。做人以後若是肯修行，也可以修成佛。那麼我今生所吃的

肉，難保不就是吃了未來佛的肉，並且現在的畜牲，在無量過去的前世中，也一定曾經做過我前生中的父母，妻子，親族，朋友，我今天吃的肉，可能就是吃我前生的父母，妻子，親族，朋友的肉了。而今我做人，它做畜牲，我吃它，我就造了殺孽，與它結下冤仇。如果被我吃的畜牲，來世它的孽債還清了，投生做了人，而我卻因為殺生造孽，投胎做畜牲，恐怕他也要報復我殺他之仇，而來殺我，吃我了。這樣說來，還能殺生麼？肉還能吃得下嗎？況且吃肉就算味道好，也不過是經過嘴裡到喉嚨那段時候，還覺得有味道，等到咽了下去，還有什麼味道？與素菜有什麼兩樣，為什麼一定要殺生造孽呢？

雖然一時做不到不吃肉，也應該漸漸地減少吃肉，直到完全不吃。這樣子慈悲心就會愈來愈增加。不但殺生應戒，就是

那些極小，不論愚蠢的或是有靈性的，凡是有生命的，都應該禁止傷害它們的性命。像要用絲來做衣服，就把蠶繭放在水裡燒，那要傷害多少蠶的性命？掘地種田，要殺害地下多少蟲的性命；想想我們穿的衣；吃的飯，是從那裡來的呢？都是殺它們的命；來養活我們自己；所以糟蹋糧食，浪費東西的罪孽，實在也應該與殺生的罪孽相等。至於隨手誤傷的生命，腳下誤踏而死的生命，又不曉得有多少，這都應該要設法防止。宋朝的蘇東坡有首詩說：愛鼠常留飯，憐蛾不點燈。

意思是說：恐怕老鼠餓死，所以為老鼠留些飯；哀憐飛蛾撲到燈上燙死，所以燈也不點。這話是多麼的仁厚慈悲呀！

善事無窮無盡，那能說得完；只要把上邊說的十件事，加以推廣發揚，那麼無數的功德，就都完備了。

【一】救濟眾人事，種類有很多，簡單而言之，大概有十種，

與人爲善一呀！愛敬存心二，成人之美三呀！勸人爲善四，救人危急五呀！與建大利六，捨財作福七呀！護持正法八，敬重尊長九呀！愛惜物命十呀，愛惜物命十。】

第四篇　謙德之效

第三篇所說的，都是積善的方法，能夠積善，自然最好，但人在社會上，不能不和人來往，做人的方法必須加以講究；而最好的方法就是謙虛了。一個人能謙虛，在社會上一定會得到大眾廣泛的支持與信任，而懂得謙虛，便更知道「日新又新」的重要；不但學問要求進步，做人做事交朋友等等，樣樣都要求進步。所有種種的好處，都從謙虛上得來，所以稱為謙德。這一篇專講謙虛的好處，謙虛的效驗；大家要仔細的研究，不可以囫圇吞棗，那就必定能夠得到大的利益。

【書經說：滿招損呀！謙受益，自滿的就要招損害。謙虛的就會受到益呀！受到益。】

易經謙卦上說：天的道理，不論什麼，凡是驕傲自滿的，

就要使他虧損，而謙虛的就讓他得到益處。地的道理，不論什

麼，凡是驕傲自滿的，也要使他改變，不能讓他永遠滿足；而

謙虛的要使他滋潤不枯，就像低的地方，流水經過，必定會充

滿了他的缺陷。鬼神的道理，凡是驕傲自滿的，就要使他受

害，謙虛的便使他受福。人的道理，都是厭惡驕傲自滿的人，

而喜歡謙虛的人。

一○四

　這樣看來，天、地、鬼、神、人、都看重謙虛的一邊。易

經上六十四卦，所講的都是天地陰陽變化的道理，教人做人的

方法。每一卦爻中，有凶有吉，凶卦是警戒人去惡從善，吉卦

是勉勵人要日新又新，唯有這個謙卦，每一爻都吉祥。書經上

也講：自滿，就會遭到損害，自謙，就會受到益處。

　我好幾次和許多人去參加考試，每次都看到貧寒的讀書

人，快要發達考中的時候，臉上一定有一片謙和，而且安詳的

光采發出來，彷彿可以用手捧住的樣子。

辛未年，我到京城去會試，我的同鄉嘉善人一起去參加會試的，大約有十個人，只有丁敬宇，這個人最年輕，而且非常謙虛，我告訴同去會試的費錦坡講：這位老兄，今年一定考中。費錦坡問我說：怎樣能看出來呢？

我說：只有謙虛的人，可以承受福報。老兄你看我們十人當中，有誠實厚道，一切事情，不敢搶在人前，像敬宇的嗎？有受人侮辱而不回答，聽到人家毀謗他而不去爭辯，像敬宇的嗎？一個人能夠做到這樣，就是天地鬼神，也都要保佑他，豈有不發達的道理？等到放榜，丁敬宇果然考中了。

丁丑年在京城裡，和馮開之住在一起，看見他總是虛心自謙，面容和順，一點也不驕傲，大大的改變了他小時候的那種

習氣。他有一位正直又誠實的朋友李霽巖，時常當面指責他的錯處，但卻只看到他，平心靜氣地接受朋友的責備，從來不反駁一句話。我告訴他說：一個人有福，一定有福的根苗；有禍，也一定有禍的預兆。只要這個心能夠謙虛，上天一定會幫助他，你老兄今年必定能夠登第了！後來馮開之果然真的考中了。

趙裕峰，名光遠，是山東省冠縣人；不滿二十歲的時候，就中了舉人，後來又考會試，卻多次不中。他的父親做嘉善縣的主任秘書，裕峰隨同他父親上任。裕峰非常羨慕嘉善縣名士錢明吾的學問，就拿自己的文章去見他，那曉得這位錢先生，竟然拿起筆來，把他的文章都塗掉了。裕峰不但不發火，並且心服口服，趕緊把自己文章的缺失改了。如此虛心用功的年輕人，實在是少有，到了明年，裕峰就考中了。

壬辰年我入京城去觀見皇帝，見到一位叫夏建所的讀書人，看到他的氣質，虛懷若谷，毫無一點驕傲的神氣，而且他那謙虛的光采，就像會逼近人的樣子。我回來告訴朋友說：凡是上天要使這個人發達，在沒有發他的福時，一定先發他的智慧，這種智慧一發，那就使浮滑的人自然會變得誠實，放肆的人也就自動收斂了，建所他溫和善良到這種地步，是已發了智慧，上天一定要發他的福了。等到放榜的時候，建所果然考中了。

江陰有一位讀書人。名叫張畏巖，他的學問積得很深，文章做得很好，在許多讀書人當中，很有名聲。甲午年南京鄉試，他借住在一處寺院裡，等到放榜，榜上沒有他的名字，他不服氣，大罵考官，眼睛不清楚，看不出他的文章好。那時候有一個道士在旁微笑，張畏巖馬上就把怒火發在道士的身上。

道士說：你的文章，一定不好。張畏巖更加的發怒說：你沒有看到我的文章，怎麼知道我寫得不好呢？道士說：我常聽人說，做文章最要緊的，是心平氣和，現在聽到你大罵考官，表示你的心非常不平，氣也太暴了，你的文章怎麼會好呢？

張畏巖聽了道士的話，倒不覺的屈服了，因此，就轉過來向道士請教。道士說：要考中功名，全要靠命，命裡不該中，文章雖好，也沒益處，仍不會考中，一定要你自己改變。

張畏巖問道：既然是命，怎樣去改變呢？道士說：造命的權，雖然在天，立命的權，還是在我；只要你肯盡力去做善事，多積陰德，什麼福不可求得呢？

張畏巖說：我是一個窮讀書人，能做什麼善事呢？道士說：行善事，積陰功，都是從這個心做出來的。只要常常存做善事，積陰功的心，功德就無量無邊了。就像謙虛這

件事，又不要花錢，你為什麼不自我反省，自己工夫太淺，不能謙虛，反而罵考官不公平呢？

張畏巖聽了道士的話，從此以後就壓低一向驕傲的志向，自己很留意把持住自己，勿走錯了路，天天加功夫去修善，天天加功夫去積德。到了丁酉年，有一天，他做夢到一處很高的房屋裡去，看到一本考試錄取的名冊，中間有許多的缺行。他看不懂，就問旁邊的人說：這是什麼？那個人說：這是今年考試錄取的名冊。而張畏巖問：為什麼名冊內有這麼多的缺行？那個人又回答說：陰間對那些考試的人，每三年考查一次，一定要積德，沒有過失，這冊裡才會有名字。像名冊前面的缺額，都是從前本該考中，但是因為他們最近犯了有罪過的事情，才把名字去掉的。

後來那個人又指了一行說：你三年來，很留心的把持住自

己，沒犯罪過，或者是應該補上這個空缺了，希望你珍重自

了凡四訓白話篇

愛，勿犯過失！果然張畏巖就在這次的會考，考中了第一百零
五名。

【造命的權在天，立命的權在我，只要肯努力，多做善事
積陰德呀！積陰德，什麼福報求不得呀？求不得？】
從上面所講的看來，舉頭三尺高，一定有神明在監察著人
的行為。因此，利人，吉祥的事情，都應該趕快的去做；凶
險，損人的事，應該避免，不要去做，這是可以由我自己決定
的，只要我存好心，約束一切不善的行為，絲毫不得罪天地鬼
神，而且還要虛心，自己肯遷就不驕傲，使得天地鬼神，時時
哀憐我，才可以有福的根基，那些滿懷傲氣的人，一定不是遠
大的器量，就算能發達，也不會長久地享受福報。稍有見識的
人，一定不肯把自己肚量，弄得很狹窄，而自己拒絕可以得到

的福，況且謙虛的人，他還有地方可以受到教導，若人不謙虛，誰肯去教他？

並且謙虛的人，肯學別人的好處，別人有善的行動，就去學他，那麼得到的善行，就沒有窮盡了。尤其是進德修業的人，一定所不可缺少的啊！

【舉頭三尺高呀！決定有神明，不但要存好心，而且要虛心，不可以做壞事，還要肯遷就，天地鬼神呀，千萬莫得罪啊！莫得罪！】

古人有幾句老話說：有心要求功名的，一定可以得到功名；有心要求富貴的，一定可以得到富貴。一個人有遠大的志向，就像樹有根一樣；樹有根，就會生出枒枝花葉來。

人要立定了這種偉大的志向，必須在每一個念頭上，都要謙虛，即使碰到像灰塵一樣極小的事情，也要使別人方便，能

夠做到這樣，自然會感動天地了。

而造福全在我自己，自己真心要造，就能夠造成。像現在那些求取功名的人，當初那有什麼真心，不過是一時的興緻罷了；興緻來了，就去求，興緻退了，就停止，孟子對齊宣王說：大王喜好音樂，若是到了極點，那麼齊國的國運大概可以興旺了。但是大王喜好音樂，只是個人在追求快樂罷了，若是能把個人追求快樂的心，推廣到與民同樂，使百姓都快樂，那麼齊國還有不興旺的麼？

我看求科名，也是這樣，要把求科名的心，落實推廣到積德行善上；並且要盡心盡力地去做，那麼命運與福報，就都能夠由我自己決定了！

各位聽眾朋友，在聽完了【了凡四訓有聲書】之後，您的內心一定是感觸很多，覺得獲益匪淺，這的的確確是一部扣人

一一二

心弦，淨化人心的有聲書；而了凡四訓這本書的原文，文字非常的優美典雅，表面上看起來，好像並不難了解，但是其中所深藏宇宙人生的道理，卻是非常的深奧，必須用心體會，才能有得於心。

所以盼望各位聽眾朋友，在聽過錄音帶以後，最好能夠熟讀了凡四訓的原文三百遍；必定能夠信心益增，效法了凡先生立命精神的決心，會更加的堅定；進而身體力行，斷惡修善。由是而個人的學業，事業，家庭均能圓滿，成聖成賢，也是指日可待的。

為了利益大眾，廣為流傳，在此我們聲明，了凡四訓有聲書並沒有所謂「智慧財產權」的問題，非常歡迎善心人士大力提倡翻錄，提供各級學校教學參考，來協助我們大、中、小學生的心理建設；並且能淨化社會人心，提昇道德觀念；大家都

學了凡精神，諸惡莫作，眾善奉行，行善積德，服務人群，如果說人人能夠如此，國家前途一定光明，世界一片祥和。

整理人的話：

各位親愛的聽眾朋友大家好，末學首先要恭喜您，能夠聽完「了凡四訓有聲書」。這是很不簡單的，如果您沒有具足相當的善根、福德、因緣，就可能沒機會聽到，甚至聽了也不能聽到心裡，內心的震動、感受，自然也不強烈；相信諸位聽完的感受一定很深、而且是法喜充滿，所以向各位祝賀。

如果您想要繼續研究「了凡四訓」，末學向各位建議，最好能夠聽「了凡四訓文教基金會」製作的當代佛門高僧，淨空法師演述的「了凡四訓講記廣播劇」錄音帶，共有十八卷，相當的精彩，並應熟讀了凡四訓原文三百遍，而且要依教奉行，如此，您對自己的命運，就有相當的把握。

中國人常講到積德，「了凡四訓」也強調行善積德，而中

國最會積德的是誰呢？就是孔子，孔子積了百代之德，所以他的子孫，七十三代的孔德成先生，以前是考試院院長；現在是總統府資政。

中國第二位會積德的就是宋朝的宰相范仲淹，范仲淹積了千年之德，所以范氏的子孫，到現在還是很興旺。所以「德」相當的重要，所謂：「有德者保之，無德者失之。」小至個人的身家性命財產，大至國家乃至全世界的存亡興廢，跟這個「德」字有相當大的因果關係，可惜一般人多未能深入的了解，而秦始皇若是知道這個道理，就不會焚書坑儒。他也想使子孫萬世而為皇，只要積德，秦朝的基業，一樣也可以保持相當的長遠；但是他不了解這個道理，所以十五年就垮了。而且子孫都很慘。這是歷史的經驗教訓，相當的發人深省。

一般人，對命運多是感到很迷茫，論語說：「不知命，無

以爲君子」，所以要知命，也不簡單。因爲這個學問很深，如果對命運眞正的了解，自然就理得心安，不可能怨天尤人了。我們現在社會上有很多亂象，各種問題層出不窮，而了凡四訓這本書，對於人心來講，有相當大的穩定作用和淨化效果。所以希望社會賢達、政府官員，都能提倡。

這個對國家社會的安定，必然會產生很大的力量，如果了凡四訓這套錄音帶，能夠有三百萬套在台灣流通，相信我們的社會風氣會爲之一變，人心道德會爲之一振，這是可以預估的。

而且這套錄音帶並沒有版權，歡迎大家助錄、弘揚；我們了凡四訓基金會成立的目的，就是希望把這本改造命運的寶典，推薦給世界上每一個人，所以將來會有英文、日文、德文，法文等各種外文的翻譯和錄音帶的出版。這對促進世界和

平、人類幸福，必定會有相當深廣的影響。

另外，了凡四訓講到布施，我們的錢財要捨，確實不容易，俗話說：「捨得捨得，有捨才有得」；韓愈講過：「一時勸人以口，百世勸人以書」。所以我們贊助了凡四訓等於是財布施，而這種財施，還有兩種的效果在裡面；就是法施和無畏施；法施是使人聞到正法，聞到正法能使人心安法喜；而遠離煩惱，心無恐怖就是無畏施也具足了。所以我們在「了凡四訓」行財布施，法施和無畏施，也都圓滿具足了！

最後希望大家給我們指教、支持、與贊助，謝謝各位！

附錄

雲谷禪師授袁了凡功過格參雲棲大師自知錄

陳癸丞　提供

准百功：

救免一人死。完一婦女節。阻人不溺一子女。為人延一嗣。

准五十功：

免墮一胎。當欲染境，守正不染。收養一無倚。葬一無主骸骨。救免一人流離。救免一人軍徒重罪。白一人冤。發一言利及百姓。

准三十功：

施一葬地與無土之家。化一為非者改行。度一受戒弟子。完聚一人夫婦。收養一無主遺棄門孩。成就一人德業。

准十功：

薦引一有德人。除一人害。編纂一切眾經法。以方術治一人重病。發至德之言。有財勢可使而不使。善遺妾婢。救一有力報人之畜命。

准五功：

勸息一人訟。傳人一保益性命事。編纂一保益性命經法。以方術救一人輕疾。勸止傳播人惡。供養一賢善人。祈福禳災等，但許善願不殺生。救一無力報人之畜命。

准三功：

受一橫不嗔。任一謗不辯。受一逆耳言。免一應責人。勸養蠶、漁人、獵人、屠人等改業。葬一自死畜類。

准二功：

讚一人善。掩一人惡。勸息一人爭。阻人一非為事。濟一人饑。留無歸人一宿。救一人寒。施藥一服。施行勸濟人書文。誦經一卷。禮懺百拜。誦佛號千聲。講演善法。諭及十人。興事利及十人。拾得遺字一千。護持僧眾一人。不拒乞人。接濟人畜一時疲頓。見人有憂，善為解慰。肉食人持齋一日。見殺不食。為己殺不食。葬一飯一僧。救一細微濕化之屬命。作功果薦沉魂。散錢粟衣帛濟死禽類。放一生。不義之財不取。代人完納債負。讓地讓產。人。饒人債負。還人遺物。不負寄托財物。建倉平糴、修造路橋、疏河掘井勸人出財作種種功德。造三寶尊像及施香燭燈油等物、施茶水、捨棺木一切方便等事。自「作功果」以下，俱以百錢為一功。、修置三寶寺院

准百過：

致一人死。失一婦女節。讚人溺一子女。絕一人嗣。

准五十過：

墮一胎。破一人婚。拋一人骸。謀人妻女。致一人流離。致一人軍徒重罪。教人不忠不孝大惡等事。發一言害及百姓。

准三十過：

造謗污陷一人。摘發一人陰私與行止事。唆一人訟。毀一人戒行。反背師長。抵觸父兄。離間人骨肉。荒年積囤五穀不糶生索。

准十過：

排擯一有德人。薦用一匪人。平人一塚。凌孤逼寡。受畜一失節婦。畜一殺眾生具。惡語向尊親、師長、良儒。修合害人毒藥。非法用刑。毀壞一切正法經典。誦經時，心中雜想惡事。以外道邪法授人。發損德之言。殺一有力報人之畜命。

准五過：

訕謗一切正法經典。見一冤可白不白。遇一病求救不救。阻絕一道路橋樑。編纂一傷化詞傳。造一渾名歌謠。惡口犯平交。殺一無力報人之畜命。

命。非法烹炮生物，使受極苦。

准三過：

嗔一逆耳言。乖一尊卑次。責一不應責人。欺誑一無識。毀人成功。見人有憂，心生暢快。見人失利、失名，心生歡喜。見人富貴，願他貧賤。失意輒怨天尤人。分外營求。

准二過：

唆一人鬪。心中暗舉惡意害人。助人為非一事。見人盜細物不阻。見人憂驚不慰。役人畜，不憐疲頓。不告人取人一針一草。遺棄字紙。暴棄五穀天物。負一約。醉犯一人。見一人饑寒不救濟。誦經差漏一字句。僧人乞食不與。拒一乞人。食酒肉五辛，誦經登三寶地。服一非法服。食一報人之畜等肉。殺一細微濕化屬命以及履巢破卵等事。背眾受利，傷用他錢。負貸。負遺。負寄托財物。因公恃勢乞索、巧索人一切財物。廢壞三寶尊像以及殿宇、器用等物。斗秤等小出大入。販賣屠刀、漁網等物。自「背眾受利」以下，俱以百錢為一過。

◎回向偈◎

願以此功德
莊嚴佛淨土
上報四重恩
下濟三途苦
若有見聞者
悉發菩提心
盡此一報身
同生極樂國

—━◆◆◆❖卍❖◆◆◆━—

了凡四訓白話篇
Liao-Fan's Four Lessons

印贈處：洛杉磯淨宗學會(Amida Socity)
地　址：5918 Cloverly Ave. Temple City, CA. 91780 U.S.A.
電　話：(626)286-5700
傳　真：(626)286-7988
網　址：http://www.amtb-la.org
淨空法師專集有聲版網址：
　　　　http://www.amtb.org.tw
承印處：台灣・福峰圖書光碟有限公司
電　話：886-2-2861-9905
傳　真：886-2-2861-7023

歡迎翻印・功德無量
公元 2005 年 1 月　敬印參仟冊

結　緣　品